MEMOIRS OF A TWENTIETH CENTURY TEACHER

MARGARET WOOD

LARGE PRINT
Oxford

Copyright © Margaret Wood, 2009

First published in Great Britain 2009
by
ISIS Publishing Ltd.

Published in Large Print 2009 by ISIS Publishing Ltd.,
7 Centremead, Osney Mead, Oxford OX2 0ES
by arrangement with
The Author

British Library Cataloguing in Publication Data
Wood, Margaret.
    Memoirs of a twentieth century teacher. - -
(Reminiscence)
    1. Wood, Margaret.
    2. Women teachers - - Great Britain - - Biography.
    3. Teachers - - Great Britain - - Biography.
    4. Large type books.
    I. Title II. Series
    371.1'0092–dc22

ISBN 978–0–7531–9532–1 (hb)
ISBN 978–0–7531–9533–8 (pb)

MEMOIRS OF A
TWENTIETH CENTURY TEACHER

To the many staff and pupils who made my years of teaching enjoyable and rewarding.

CONTENTS

FORWARD

I was at school myself from 1935 to 1946. During this time, the 1944 Education Act was formulated and partly implemented.

I taught from the early 1950s until the late 1980s so I encountered many educational changes, the semi-abolition of the 11+ examination, the introduction of the comprehensive system and the raising of the school leaving age.

I taught business related subjects, including office skills, to 11–18 year olds in a wide variety of schools — Secondary Technical, Secondary Grammar, Secondary Modern, Comprehensive — and in Further Education, teaching in the south west and north west of England.

For most of my teaching career I was also an external examiner, encountering the many changes which took place during this period, not least the introduction of CSE (Certificate of Secondary Education) and later GCSE (General Certificate of Secondary Education) examinations.

By the end of the century, there had been much debate about the 'dumming down' of external examinations. As a Chief Examiner, I tried, quite unsuccessfully, to maintain the high standards by which British qualifications had been held worldwide.

My career, both in teaching and in examining, provided me with a wealth of unusual and often amusing situations. It is these which I seek to share with my readers.

CHAPTER
ONE

Evening Classes

I gained my first teacher's diploma, The Incorporated Phonographic Society's Typewriting Teachers' Diploma, in 1950, aged nineteen years and was given an intermediate typewriting evening class of adults to teach the following year.

I guess my somewhat extrovert personality and, perhaps sometimes, overconfidence in my ability, helped to overcome my youthful looks. Suffice to say that I enjoyed several years of teaching evening classes before I began teaching full-time day students.

My first lesson was not without a hitch. On arriving for the class, I was given a student registration form by the receptionist who took some convincing that I was, in fact, the teacher of the class and required the class register.

Ever prepared, I had arrived early enough to write some notes on the chalkboard so that students could be gainfully employed copying them until everyone was settled and ready for the lesson to begin. Alas my efforts were in vain. When students didn't seem too keen to follow my instructions of, "Just copy up the notes from the board until we are sure everyone is present and I can begin," the reason was soon made apparent. The neat, small handwriting was legible only from the first two rows of the class. I soon learned to check the legibility of my writing prior to the entrance of pupils in future classes.

Another lesson, again well prepared, was to demonstrate how to use an ink duplicator. Unfortunately, I did not possess a qualification as an electrician and proceeded to plug the AC electrical plug of the new duplicator into a DC socket. The result was to plunge the whole building into darkness, necessitating the termination of all classes for that evening and students being sent home early. Fortunately, although the blown fuses were eventually traced and replaced, it was never discovered who had caused the problem.

My next acquisition was that of the Royal Society of Arts Teachers' Certificate in Pitman's Shorthand. Once again I was given an intermediate evening class of adults to teach. Three of the students in this class were the wife of the Director of Education and two of her friends. They had enrolled for the course by way of refreshing their knowledge acquired whilst still at school.

I approached the class with the full knowledge that I had prepared well and would not be intimidated by the presence of "VIPs".

"Excuse me, but I don't think you've got that right."

As was the custom after a piece of dictation, I was putting the difficult outlines on the board and explaining the rule behind them. I checked the outline and was convinced it was correct.

"Let's leave that for a minute; I'll go over it again later," I retorted, playing for time.

My explanation was accepted, and we moved on to another piece of dictation for which I again put shorthand outlines on the board for the difficult words only to have my competence called into question by these ladies.

At break time, I decided to confront these students in an attempt to clear up the matter, for I now had some idea what the cause might be.

"Ladies, I am sorry we seem to be at variance with our knowledge of Pitman's shorthand, but I think I may have the explanation. When did you learn shorthand?"

"When we were at school".

"I presume that was a few years ago," I surmised.

"Of course."

"Then you will have learned the Classic Pitman's shorthand. The system was thoroughly upgraded only a couple of years ago, and a somewhat simplified version called the New Era was introduced. It is that system which I am teaching. I think you will find that the rules you and I cannot agree upon are those which have been changed with the new version."

Sure enough, this was the reason, and the rest of the term passed without question as to my knowledge of the subject, and the ladies were all successful in their external examinations.

My expertise in the teaching of shorthand was to take an even further "knock" when I was appointed to teach army personnel at a local RAF airbase which had been taken over by the Americans.

My students, all male members of the American armed forces, had been coerced into taking shorthand and typewriting lessons so that they could progress to clerical positions on the base.

My first shorthand lesson followed a similar pattern to that of the evening class. Once again, the students didn't seem to be following the same system as I was teaching. It soon became clear that Pitman's shorthand was seldom taught in America. The few students of my class who had any knowledge of shorthand had learned Gregg's shorthand at school. Those new to the subject were keen to learn a system which would also be useful in civilian life. This time, I had to admit defeat. The two systems were so different that I would have been hard pushed to try to learn the system and teach it at the same time. The idea of teaching shorthand in England was abandoned, and extra typewriting and office practice lessons were introduced.

CHAPTER
TWO

Day-time Teaching

I gained my first teaching diploma, for the teaching of typewriting, in 1950. The stint of teaching evening classes convinced me to abandon my dream of becoming an actress and pursue a new career as a teacher.

Having no grammar school education, I knew that obtaining qualified teacher status was going to be difficult and may need lots of further study, but I saw an opportunity into this hallowed profession through my office skills.

In 1951, I applied for, and was successful in gaining, a full-time teaching post with the American armed forces stationed at RAF Fairford, a small but important airfield in the Cotswolds, quite close to my home town of Swindon.

My contract stated that I had to teach four two-hour periods each day for five days a week. The salary was exceptional, much higher than I was receiving as a secretary. My evening class teaching had been two-hourly sessions so I thought nothing of the contract. However, working from 8a.m. to 5p.m., with one hour for lunch, was quite demanding, especially as the large numbers of students (some twenty to each class) generated quite a lot of marking. I also had to take into account the journey to work. Fortunately, the American Army arranged transport with one of their personnel who lived "off base" in Swindon, motoring to Fairford daily. I cycled to his house each morning, arriving at 7a.m. We were at the base in plenty of time for my first class.

The homeward journey was not as precise. Inevitably my driver insisted on calling, en route, at the PX (the equivalent of our NAFFI) in order to purchase a bottle of whiskey, which I held during the journey home so that he could take regular swigs.

This rather arduous teaching position gave me the impetus to start gaining further qualifications so that I could eventually teach in English state schools. It also provided me with some amusing incidents and opened my eyes to another country's culture.

One of my students, an army sergeant, often arrived in class late and was clearly wearing his pyjamas under his uniform, for a good two inches of the striped material could be perceived below each trouser leg. This sergeant also had a temper. He would rant and rave at other students who arrived before him and grabbed the best typewriters. The machines had been hired from a local firm but were mostly in good condition and of the same make — Underwood. This made teaching much easier than in the evening classes where various makes of machines were used.

One morning, the sergeant arrived late, as usual, and had missed the instructions I had given for completing a rather intricate piece of work. Things did not go well for him, and he quickly lost his temper. This culminated in the expletive, "This bloody Limey typewriter."

Thinking that his next move might be to hurl the said machine through the nearby window, I quickly moved to his side, turned the machine around and pointed to the back on which was inscribed, "Made in USA".

The sergeant was somewhat subdued and resorted to swearing at his own inability to cope with the work, rather than blaming his "tools".

My eyes were opened to the racial tension prevalent at this time. When the men entered the room, the white men came in first and sat near the front of the class. The black men all sat at the back. There was virtually no communication between the two sets of students.

I spent nearly a year teaching at this American base but eventually decided to apply for a part-time teaching post at a Secondary Technical School in Swindon.

The 1950s and 60s was a time of great change in educational organisation. As far back as the 1944 Education Act, the raising of the school leaving age from fourteen years had been planned, and, by 1950, the Technical School had emerged whereby vocational subjects could be taught for the final two years of compulsory elementary education.

The local education authority agreed to pay me a salary commensurate with that of teaching in evening classes, hence, the salary was quite good, but I did not qualify for holiday pay or other fringe benefits and could only be employed on a part-time basis. This turned out to be a very good way to approach my newfound profession.

The pupils, at this Secondary Technical School, were aged between 13 and 15 years and, by dint of the prospective career opportunities, it was mainly girls who studied office skills. I was employed to teach shorthand and office studies.

Unfortunately, the school was located at The Lawns, an open space which comprised several Nissan huts dotted about amid a sea of mud. The commercial department shared facilities with the building department where boys studied building crafts prior to embarking on apprenticeships. Areas where cement had been mixed for the bricklaying course merged quite easily with the grassy paths of the summer and the sea of mud in the winter.

Heating was provided in each hut by a wood-burning stove. This provided very adequate heat so long as one remembered to keep the stove well fuelled and the caretaker remembered to deliver sufficient wood for the day. The huts were draughty. The unfortunate pupils seated by a window or the back door, usually froze during the winter months.

However, this was to be one of the best teaching positions I had. The children, although categorized as 11+ failures, were most receptive. They could appreciate the opportunity of obtaining good employment if they were proficient in office skills. They worked hard and faired well. The staff were terrific. The head was also the head of the building department, a short, fat man who was a great disciplinarian yet adored by his students. He respected and supported the staff and was sympathetic to the adversities encountered in such an alien teaching environment. Fortunately for me, the reorganisation of secondary education in the Swindon area meant that office skills subjects were now to be taught in existing schools, and the Technical School was duly closed.

In their wisdom, the local education authority decided that office skills would now be taught in the two grammar schools of the town. This was probably because a new "O" level examination had been introduced. This was the first vocational "O" level and was called Commercial Subjects. To obtain a pass, students had to pass in two of three subjects, shorthand, typewriting or accounts.

The cost of providing typewriters for each school was prohibitive, so it was decided to offer shorthand and accounts in both the grammar schools and pupils would be entered for this new "O" level in those two subjects only.

I was successful in being appointed the part-time teacher of shorthand, dividing my time between the two schools. To my great surprise, my colleague, the person appointed to teach accounts, was my old Head of Department when I was studying at the local Day Commercial Classes during my own final two years of education.

The experience of teaching in grammar schools was quite opposite to anything I had experienced so far. To start with, I was greeted by the first headmaster with,

"Ah! You must be the new teacher for shorthand. Well, let me tell you now that I don't want you in my school. I don't want vocational subjects taught here. I have been forced to accept this change in the curriculum. Here is your timetable; these are your pupils. Don't ask me for extra periods on the timetable. There are none."

It was quite evident, from the pupils in my classes, that they had been deemed the "rejects" of the academic environment in which they found themselves. There seemed to be as many boys as girls. Few of the boys could see themselves in office posts and certainly did not see the need to learn shorthand.

I asked one girl why she had chosen to study shorthand and accounts for "O" level. She replied, "At the end of the third year, several of us were called together and told we were no good at most subjects so would be starting this new course."

Limited timetabled lessons, less able students and a restriction on the number of subjects offered meant that success at "O" level was never likely to be attained, but several girls benefited from the experience and did, eventually, obtain worthwhile employment in offices.

As for me, teaching in a grammar school was an education in itself, having never been privy to such an establishment in my own schooling.

The first "eye opener" was the staff. From the friendly, almost family-type environment of the small staffroom in the Secondary Technical School where staff had supported each other through many adversities, not least the lack of heat and the muddy conditions, I was plunged into a large and very divisive staff. There were two staffrooms, one for the ladies and one for the men.

The ladies' room was presided over by the Deputy Head with a title of Doctor. She had her own chair and always took a nap during the lunch-hour break. During this time, everyone spoke in whispers. It amazed us that she always awoke exactly five minutes before the bell for afternoon lessons was rung.

She ruled all the female staff with a rod of iron. We were told not to wear tights and to ensure that the seams of our stockings were always straight. On one occasion, she admonished us for wearing headscarves to school. Apparently hats were more feminine. I hadn't worn a hat since my honeymoon, so I always arrived at school bare-headed, despite the weather.

All the staff wore academic gowns, except the part-time teachers of commercial subjects who, by nature of their professions, had not been awarded university degrees. The only other exceptions were the PE staff who needed to be more suitably attired for their job.

The Senior Master had a room of his own. I was once allowed in there to use his telephone but reminded beforehand not to move anything.

"If he finds a single sheet of paper out of place, he will go mad," I was warned. My telephone call was swift, for I felt I was on hallowed ground.

Needless-to-say, the staff were not welcoming of the two new part-time staff foisted upon them to oversee this "totally inappropriate" addition to their grammar-school curriculum. Unfortunately, timetable constraints meant that I seldom saw my counterpart, since accounts lessons were invariably at different times from my shorthand lessons.

Added to my problems was the fact that I had to devote my time between two grammar schools situated several miles apart. With no car, I spent endless hours waiting for buses to take me to the other establishment in order to conduct a half hour lesson.

The timetable constraints, the academically poor pupils and lack of support from the Head and staff of the school soon confirmed that I was not going to be able to get the pupils up to "O" level standard within the two year course so, after about eighteen months, I applied for a part-time teaching post at a Secondary Modern school which had begun to introduce commercial subjects.

Again — what a difference. The pupils were drawn from the more able, since commercial subjects were seen to be an introduction to well-paid office jobs. The pupils were keen and the staff anxious to boost examination results by entering pupils for various skills examinations, mainly offered by The Royal Society of Arts or Pitmans.

This was an all-girls school, so the staff were all female. By and large, they were a friendly bunch of ladies. Several had small children of their own. One day, one of the teachers brought her two-year-old into the staff room before school, prior to delivering her to the nursery opposite the school. Sitting on the table, the child exclaimed, "Oh, Mummy, that's cold. I've got no knickers on!"

The mother was not at all perturbed. She merely excused herself from first lesson so that she could "pop into Marks and Spencers to buy some knickers"! Apparently this was not an uncommon occurrence. She had previously brought the child to school with odd socks and odd shoes.

I remember one mid-morning break at this school. Being new to the staffroom, I was not aware that older members had their own chairs. The PE teacher entered the room, looked in my direction and then almost threw a fit.

"She's in my chair! I need to sit down. I've just had netball with 4B, and now I have to take another PE class. I must sit down."

With several empty chairs in the room, I couldn't understand the outburst until I realized that all eyes were on me and guessed I was the culprit of some great misdemeanour. I quickly vacated said chair and never sat there again.

I spent some happy and successful months at this school until the local education authority decided, once again, to reorganize secondary education in the town.

CHAPTER
THREE

Times they are a-changing

The report by the Central Advisory Council for Education in England entitled "Half Our Future", published in 1963, proposed many new initiatives for education. The aim was to establish schools which would best suit the needs of the pupils.

The proposed recommendations included an immediate raising of the school leaving age to sixteen years for all pupils entering secondary education from September 1965, and the provision of "a range of courses broadly related to occupational interest, for pupils in the fourth and fifth years of a five-year course".

Indeed, the report went on to suggest that touch typewriting might be taught as a general subject since it may be deemed a skill for life. This gave me renewed hope that my services would be in demand for the foreseeable future.

The report also made recommendations for changes in teacher training which were, eventually, to lead to my being able to embark on a two-year mature student teacher-training course and so gain qualified teacher status.

At the time of this report, success at the 11+ examination was still compulsory for entry to grammar schools. Sadly, many parents had their children coached for this examination which resulted in many young people being wrongly sent to these academically geared establishments. Their inability to cope with the pressures of such a demanding curriculum meant that they fell behind and, as was evident from my experience with the grammar-school pupils designated to study commercial subjects, they were branded as failures by the age of fourteen.

For those who failed the 11+ examination, secondary modern schools became their establishment for the final years of schooling. With the school leaving age raised to fifteen years (and the proposed further raising to sixteen years), schools had pupils long enough to ensure they gave them the best and most appropriate education for their future employment.

Several pupils at secondary modern schools were late developers, and so these schools creamed off their brightest pupils and allowed them to take "O" levels. Since the abolition of matriculation and higher schools certificates as the ultimate of the grammar schools, "O" level examinations had been introduced which could be taken as single subjects, building into the five or more deemed necessary for entrance to further education courses including the "A" level examinations required for university entrance.

By the end of the 1960s, the idea of comprehensive schools for all pupils, regardless of ability, was gaining the support of many local education authorities. In my own area, it was decided to adopt the Leicestershire plan which meant the abolition of the 11+ and grammar schools, with all children transferring, at the age of eleven, to a junior high school and then, at the age of fourteen, to a senior high school which would cater for their tuition through to school leaving or entry to higher education.

I was, currently, employed part-time in another secondary school where I was able to teach typewriting throughout the curriculum for the final two years of schooling, together with associated subjects such as office practice and commerce. Shorthand and accounts were also offered in some secondary modern schools, especially where pupils opted to stay on into a sixth year to take "O" levels or (in a few schools) "A" levels.

My experience of teaching in this school helped me enormously. Besides the vocational aspect of my subjects, I was given classes of less able pupils, deemed non-examination groups, who would seek to leave school at the earliest opportunity (fifteen years), prior to taking any external examinations. I like to believe that teaching touch typing to such pupils gave them added manual dexterity which could be put to good use in any workplace which necessitated the operation of machinery.

With this new education for all at secondary level, there developed a new type of examination — the CSE (Certificate of Secondary Education). The idea of this examination was to cater for all secondary modern (later comprehensive) school pupils who were not capable of "O" levels. Although of a lower demand than an "O" level paper, success at Grade I was deemed to be equivalent to a C grade at "O" level in that subject. Those who were not awarded a Grade I could still pass the CSE at lower levels from grades 2–6.

It was at this time that I became really interested in external examining. I had been marking Pitman Typewriting examinations for some years and enjoyed the work, although it was not highly paid. This new examination meant that, at first, teachers were in charge of marking much of their own candidates' work. They then met at local centres to talk with other teacher-examiners and the chief examiner in order to moderate their work.

This again was quite an eye-opener for me. I had met few commercial subject teachers before and was appalled when confronted with some of the work presented from other schools. Marking had been rather slipshod. Many typing errors had been missed. Some teachers had purposely marked all errors in pencil, knowing that these would be less obvious than the red pen marks on the candidate's work. Other teachers argued endlessly about what was considered correct or acceptable practice, particularly in regard to letter layout and display work.

I was now hooked on examination standards and determined to make my mark as an external examiner.

As far as employment was concerned, the Local Education Authority decided to reorganize secondary education. Secondary Modern schools became Junior High schools catering for pupils from eleven to fourteen years of age. The Grammar schools became

Senior High schools to which pupils transferred at fourteen, remaining there until the end of their education, at sixteen years, or until embarking on higher education at eighteen years.

I was now asked to transfer from the Junior High school to the neighbouring Senior High school in order to prepare pupils for various commercial subject examinations at CSE. The Junior High school Head was loathe to see me leave and to have his successful vocational courses and their resources transferred to the Senior High school. To my horror, the school to which I was transferred was one of the Grammar schools at which I had been made so unwelcome just a year or so ago. This time the staff, and the Head, were just as displeased at having a whole new generation of pupils to cater for, including less academically able students of which few teachers had experience. Indeed it was ironic that the classics teacher from the old grammar school, finding his subject in decline, was put in charge of the less able, non-examination group.

Pupils suffered somewhat in the transitional period. Many grammar school teachers were totally unprepared for teaching at lower levels and discipline was often a problem.

I remember gazing out of the staffroom window during a free period and looking into a hutted annex where the class was in uproar. I alerted the Deputy Head to the situation. She proceeded to visit the class in order to ascertain the cause of such mayhem. She found the teacher, crouching behind the upturned teacher's desk, taking refuge from a class of fourteen-year-olds who were totally beyond control.

From my point of view, I quickly learned that incidents of indiscipline were not always quelled by the teacher raising his or her voice.

I had been taking my form register one afternoon, when there was a tremendous noise coming from the corridor outside the classroom. The noise was made by what seemed like hundreds of pupils waiting to occupy my classroom and others in the vicinity. Shouts, from me, of, "Be quiet out there" did little to quell the commotion.

All of a sudden there was silence.

I finished taking the register and opened the classroom door. There, standing among the rabble of pupils, was a six foot tall ex-policemen turned teacher, holding a very long window pole. His air of calm, accompanied by this lethal weapon, had been enough to hush the most violent of crowds. From that day onwards, I learned to adopt an imposing stance and a sinister glare when faced with indiscipline among pupils.

As with my previous experience in the Grammar schools, I found a certain group of students, deemed too undisciplined or too intellectually incapable, were guided towards opting for commercial subjects. Where these pupils, particularly the boys, had been wrongly advised about their options, it took all of my guile and experience to control the class. However, I did also have large numbers, mostly girls, who were very motivated and keen to succeed in these worthwhile subjects. External examinations were developing, and there were now plenty of vocational examinations for them to aspire to.

The transfer of pupils at the age of fourteen was not without its difficulties. The Junior High schools had had pupils for three years and were aware of pockets of pupils prone to unruly behaviour. It was deemed that such pupils should transfer to the senior school without blemish on their character so that they may be given "a new start" in the new environment.

There was one occasion when this did not work favourably. Before the start of teaching a new year, there was a staff meeting at which teachers were given details of the tutorial group for which they would be responsible and their teaching timetables. At one such meeting we were told that the Junior High school had identified two particular troublemakers, each boy successfully recruiting gangs of boys to support them.

"It's important that these two boys are kept well apart. They should not be in the same tutorial group, house group, and, as far as possible, not taught in the same classes."

The Head read out the names of the two boys and, low and behold, both had been allocated to my tutorial group. Fortunately this situation was rectified prior to the commencement of term, but I must admit to having a hard time with the one remaining boy in my group.

Both the Junior and Senior High schools ran house systems. Competition between the houses was keen, especially in the area of sporting activities. I had never been a supporter of the house system and felt rather responsible for the fact that, on entering the Junior High school, I had been put into Neptune House which had been the top house for some years. The first year of my being a member, the house plunged to the bottom. Although I took no responsibility for this, I did feel that my presence was somewhat of a "jinx".

On relocating to the Senior High school, I was put into Schweitzer House (named after Albert Schweitzer). Within a month Albert Schweitzer was dead. Now I really was starting to feel paranoid and pledged to give the house system only mild support.

With the problems of reorganization and the fact that the town itself had been designated an expanding, overspill town, it was inevitable that the school was over-subscribed. Vocational courses were particularly over-subscribed especially when some of the ex-grammar school pupils, who were not coping well academically, decided to opt for commercial courses. Added to this, the Head wisely suggested that typewriting could be offered to all sixth-form pupils since such a skill would inevitably be of advantage to them in producing a thesis when they were at university.

I remember having to teach typewriting in a corridor. For one hour a week, some ten sixth-form students had to carry a typewriter from a nearby store cupboard and set it up on a desk outside the RE (religious education) room.

At this time, it was thought prudent to teach keyboarding skills by the use of music. There were some excellent "Typing to Music" records available, but I hit on the idea that, so long as the pupils understood the need for a regular beat to the music (usually present in the current pop music) they could bring in their own favourite pop music for use in part of each lesson. The pupils thrived. They enjoyed their lessons and progressed rapidly. The same cannot be said for the RE class, although I must admit that the teacher was most cooperative and only occasionally requested that we "turn the music down a bit."

One good thing came out of the transformation of this old grammar school into a comprehensive — the large staffroom became a mixed room. The old "ladies" staffroom was turned into a quiet room into which teachers could retire to do some marking away from the usual banter of a large, mixed staff. Away went the need for staff to wear gowns. It was evident that most of the new staff, transferring from the Secondary Modern schools, were teacher trained but without degrees. A few of the "old" staff wore gowns at all times, and the Head insisted all those with a degree must wear the relevant gown at the annual Prize Giving Ceremony. This proved quite divisive and, I am sure, would not be tolerated in today's climate.

I stayed at this school for about four years, during which time I gained the relevant "O" and "A" level qualifications so that I could gain acceptance to the mature students' teacher training course which I undertook from 1968–1970.

The Head of this "new" type of school eventually became very supportive, and I owe him much for his encouragement to achieve qualified teacher status. He even kept my old job open for me during my two year absence and allowed me to use his school for my final teaching practice. On taking up my appointment again he promptly gave me a graded post in recognition of my usefulness to the school and my responsibility in introducing these new courses.

Sadly, I soon had to leave this school. A change in my husband's career necessitated a family move to the north west of England.

CHAPTER
FOUR

Culture Shock

Having never lived north of "Watford Gap", the family's move to the north west of England was somewhat of a culture shock.

We bought a house in the Lancashire seaside resort of Southport, and, after finding suitable schools for our three teenage children, I set about getting myself a job.

I applied for a post as Deputy Head of Lower School in a Catholic Comprehensive school in Newton-le-Willows. The interview could have been rather demanding since the interviewing panel consisted mainly of priests. However, I was to encounter my first experience of northern humour.

One of the first questions at the interview was, "Why have you moved from the west country to Lancashire?"

I was a little reluctant, but had to explain that my husband's new position was that of Personnel Director for Littlewoods Pools. I thought the priests would not approve of this employer. I need not have worried. The next question, from an elderly priest, was, "What's the chance of you getting a winning coupon into Littlewoods after the results are declared?"

I presumed the question had been asked in jest and proffered only a wry smile as an answer.

I was offered the job and began another interesting period in my teaching career. It was explained that a shortage of teachers had meant that most of the staff were non-Catholics, hence, as a practising Catholic, I would be expected to teach RE. I was not qualified to do so and found that area of the curriculum quite daunting. Secondly, as my role was that of Deputy Head of the Lower School, I would not be teaching commercial subjects since these were reserved for the upper school pupils. I would be teaching English and Environmental Studies (the latter as part of a team).

Appreciating that my main function was to help lead the lower school pupils, I accepted my new timetable and set about getting to know the younger pupils. This was not easy. A knock at my door resulted in a distraught eleven year old requesting, "Please, Miss, can you lend me some dinner money. I forgot my butties."

I had to admit to the child that I did not understand the term "butties".

"Sarnies," was her frustrated attempt to make this totally illiterate new teacher understand her.

When the next pupil was in fear of detention because he had forgotten his "pumps" and another that he had torn his "kecks", I realized that northern folk spoke a different language which I had better make haste to learn.

Northern folk are deemed to be friendly. My daughter, herself suffering from this change of culture, remarked quite innocently, "You know, Mum, that they say northerners are friendly. I think they are just nosey."

Although the staff at the school were quite friendly, it was obvious that I was an alien among them. Many times I was told that, being able to afford a house in Southport, I had no idea what it was like to live, as these pupils did, in working-class communities. Constant reminders that I came from a working-class background myself did little to convince the children and my teaching colleagues of my own humble beginnings.

The school adopted a policy of mixed-ability teaching. I found this quite difficult. I knew that I could teach children of all abilities, but I did like them in groups of like-minded recipients of knowledge. Added to this, the Head was very demanding. Forecast books containing details of all lessons to be taught during the coming week had to be on his desk on Monday morning. On Friday morning, record books had to be handed in. With duties as a Deputy Head, teaching subjects for which I was not trained and to younger pupils than I was used to, meant that I stayed only six months at this school. It had been an experience but one which I did not want to repeat. I knew that my talents lay in teaching older pupils commercial subjects, and so I applied for, and was appointed to, my first Head of Department post at another comprehensive school, this time in a small town just north of Southport.

I relished the chance to run my own department, albeit it comprised me and just two other part-time teachers. I was given the chance to expand the number of commercial subjects taught in the school and introduced both commerce and accounts, in addition to the office skills.

Since the school only catered for 11–16 year olds, I was also appointed to visit local Further Education establishments, Sixth Form colleges and Grammar schools in the area to ascertain what they offered in the way of "A" levels or vocational courses should our school leavers wish to transfer to them in order to continue their education. I gleaned much useful information about courses and schools by this part of my job.

My only skirmish with a recalcitrant pupil in this well-disciplined school was when I deemed that a girl had been cheeky to me. I reported the incident to the Deputy Head who brushed it aside with the explanation, "Oh, she comes from Banks. Banks people are a funny lot."

I knew that Banks was an area of Southport, but I never did find out how such people were "funny".

One favourable aspect of this move from the Newton-le-Willows school was the travelling from home to school. To get to Newton-le-Willows, I had to drive some twenty miles to the M6 motorway, travel south for a few miles, then go through the town itself. In winter, fog was a great hazard, particularly until the M6 was reached. The return journey was inevitably made during rush hour, since I was seldom able to leave school at the end of the afternoon session.

At this new school, I motored some fifteen miles each way but mostly along the coastal road beside the Mersey estuary with Blackpool Tower in the distance. In winter, the drive was idyllic and relaxing even though the wind, gusting up the Mersey, made control of the car on the exposed road quite hazardous. In the summer, I encountered quite a different hazard. Early holiday makers thronged the beach and wandered aimlessly across the road to the Pleasure Beach Amusement Park opposite. The slow progress and constant emergency stops put several minutes on my journey and ensured I arrived home with frazzled nerves.

After three years in the northwest, my husband's job necessitated a move back to the south.

CHAPTER
FIVE

North to South

"Well, what was your first day like?" This was a simple enough question from my husband at the close of my first day as Head of Commerce at a large outer London comprehensive school.

"Put it like this . . . the staff, all 91 of them, are very nice, the classrooms and equipment reasonable, but the children are horrible. The trouble is, there are over one thousand of them."

On applying for posts in the south, I had taken into account the fact that my husband's job was in London, and the family sought to relocate somewhere west of that great city.

I had no previous experience of teaching in the capital and certainly appreciated the salary offered. As Head of Department, I would receive a Scale 5 graded post — the highest grade for a Head of Department — plus London weighting allowance.

Two posts were available, one in a girls' school and one in a co-ed comprehensive in an outer London borough. The latter appealed to me, and I was successful in my application.

My husband and I rented a small flat in Maida Vale in London from which we could both motor to our respective jobs. We had to leave two of our children at home in Southport until they had taken their "O" and "A" level examinations respectively. This meant a five hundred mile round trip each weekend to visit them, do the housework, washing and ironing in order to leave things ready for the next week.

But the worst part of the move, from my point of view, was the journey from our flat in London to the suburbs of west London. I had never driven in London, and the first day's journey was attempted with some trepidation. Suffice to say, I negotiated the back street plan which had been drawn up for me until I arrived at the elevated section of the M4 motorway for the final part of the journey. My first day of teaching was spent wondering if, and how, I would find my way home.

As I have explained, the members of staff at this new school were delightful and very friendly although, being quite a tough school, it did suffer with a rapid staff turnover. With over 90 members of staff, I decided I would take note of up to ten teachers each week and get to know their names and positions in the school. This was not a good idea. It seemed that, as soon as I got to know someone, they left. Added to this, I realized it was important to get to know the Heads of the four houses since they seemed to know the troublemakers among the pupils — the majority of which seemed to have chosen to study commercial subjects.

As Head of Department, I was in charge of the other staff, just two part-time ladies who had valiantly held the department together until a new Head could be appointed.

For my first lesson I decided I would relieve the over-stretched typing teacher of some of her pupils and give them their first lesson in commerce, a subject which had been neglected since the retirement of the previous Head of Department some six months previously. I asked the typing teacher to send me those pupils considered "overspill" to her class. In hindsight, this was my first mistake. She obviously picked out all the troublesome pupils to send to me.

I had prepared a simple but interesting lesson and had purchased a new set of attractive commerce textbooks. The pupils ambled into the room. The first group crowded into the back desks, starting loud conversations as they did so. The rest spread out around the middle of the room, slouching into seats in an attitude of "We're not interested".

Everything I said to the class received an uncomplimentary retort from the back row — a group of fifteen-year-old girls with strong cockney accents and statures well above my meagre 5'2". Attempts to cajole them into work failed. Ignoring their wisecracks failed. I was at a loss.

I put a series of tasks on the chalkboard, ensured all had writing implements and a textbook and sat at the front of the class hoping some pupils would attempt the set work. Not a jot was written. No book was opened. The girls got themselves into small groups and chatted, noisily, about their social lives. Another instruction on the board to the effect, "When you decide you want to be quiet and take part in the lesson, please let me know" was also ignored.

I had been teaching for twenty years in a variety of schools, and I had never been unable to discipline a class, however unruly. I began to think that, if this was what life was to be like, I didn't want to continue teaching, even at this fantastically lucrative salary. I sat at my desk, opened a newspaper and ignored the mayhem.

Some ten minutes later, the Deputy Head entered the room and asked the reason for the noise.

"They are unteachable," I explained, "so I have given up."

"Who are the ringleaders?" she enquired.

I selected five or six large, vociferous girls from the back row.

"Take yourselves down to the Head's study. Your teacher will follow," she instructed.

I left her in charge of a somewhat subdued class and followed the ringleaders down to the Head's study. I had met him at my interview and found him to be a very quietly spoken, real gentleman. I was sceptical about his ability to deal with these girls and solve my problem.

"Do come in," he said. "Now, what seems to be the problem?"

I tried to be fair in explaining that the girls had been taken from a typing lesson, which they enjoyed, and asked to start a new subject called commerce, a subject which would be essential if I was to develop this small department into a thriving part of the school and boost the school's successes at "O" and "A" level examinations.

The girls endeavoured to interject on several occasions, to explain that they didn't want to learn any new subjects. They were going to leave school as soon as they were fifteen so wouldn't be taking any external examinations. Such interruptions were greeted with a stoney stare from the Head who never allowed them a chance to put their side of the story.

I finished my explanation with, "This is the worst set of pupils I have come across in over twenty years of teaching in a wide variety of schools. I do not intend to return to this school tomorrow."

At this, the Head rose from behind his desk, took up a cane (which I later learned he had had no intention of using), strutted forcefully in front of the group announcing in a loud, menacing tone, "It has taken me six months to find a replacement for the Head of Department who retired last year. The existing staff have attempted to keep the department running so that we could find a teacher worthy of developing the department. We have found such a teacher, and this is the way you treat her. If I can persuade her to return to school tomorrow, you will apologize for your misconduct, you will attend her classes, obey her orders and make an attempt to achieve success before you leave this school. The alternative course of action is for me to exclude you from this moment. Your parents will be informed, and you will not be allowed back into this school . . . ever. Is that clear?"

Mumbled replies indicated that, maybe, I would not have any more trouble with this group. This skirmish went some way to teaching me how to handle this new type of pupil.

I decided that I would see the rest of the day out and, if I returned tomorrow, I would seek the attitudes of other members of staff to these recalcitrant pupils.

I returned to school the next day and, during mid-morning break, spoke to several members of staff about my experience with the ringleaders of my troublesome class. Their comments assured me that this group was notorious throughout the school. One young graduate teacher enquired, "Was Donna among that group?"

"Yes," I replied.

"Well, if you got her to sit on a chair, you did well. For my first lesson with her, she insisted on dancing on the top of the desk."

One of the Heads of House tried to excuse another of the girl's behaviour by explaining, "She has an awful home life, you know. Her mother is a belly dancer in Soho."

Quite what that had to do with her class behaviour was lost on me, but I soon got to know of other students whose home life left much to be desired. Whilst Heads of Houses were often willing to accept less than good behaviour from such pupils, I was determined to insist on maintaining my high standards of class discipline — essential for my survival, apart from anything else.

In the course of the next few weeks, the typing teacher explained that she had applied for the Head of Department post but, not being a qualified teacher, had been turned down. Despite this, she had agreed to double up her typing classes in order to keep the department together. Sensing her disappointment, I could see her reason for selecting the unruly element of her large class to give to the naïve new teacher — a baptism of fire would prepare her for the task ahead, not only in running the department but developing it as the Head envisaged.

The other part-time member of the department was also unqualified but doing quite a good job of teaching even the less-motivated girls. She was a slightly built lady with a gentle manner. Unfortunately, she also taught some of the girls which had made up my first class.

Not many weeks into my first term, this teacher came to me near to tears. She had reprimanded one of the girls for refusing to do any work. This girl had become very confrontational ending with her leaving the room calling over her shoulder, "I've had enough of you. I'm going to get my brother up here. He'll soon teach you that you can't boss me around."

With the Head's permission, I allowed the teacher to leave school early that day to avoid any confrontation outside the school gates. I was left to supervise the class for the rest of the lesson. The pupils were agog with explanations.

"You did the right thing, there, Miss. You should see her brothers. They're a right family. Everybody on the estate is scared of them."

It transpired that another girl from this group had been sacked from her Saturday job in a local chicken factory because she took a carving knife to a fellow employee who had made an insensitive remark to her.

Suffice to say that the majority of other classes I taught were trouble free. The part-time typing teacher took early retirement shortly after my appointment. The other part-timer left soon after the incident in which she had been threatened.

CHAPTER
SIX

New Staff — New Subjects

I was now left to hold the department together until new staff could be appointed. However, at my interview, I had clearly set out my plans for the department. I intended to expand it away from the provision of office skills for the less-able girls of the school to a department which would cater for all abilities to study a full range of business subjects to "A" level examination standard. Indeed, I had made it a condition of my appointment that I would have access to pupils across the ability range when options for courses were discussed at the end of the third year.

This was a breakthrough in commercial education. Most schools guided pupils into commercial studies because they were not academically capable of studying to "A" level and because there were plenty of junior office jobs available at that time. My understanding of a co-ed comprehensive system was that it should provide equal opportunities for all. I was determined to ensure this was so and was lucky to be in a school which was prepared to base its ideology on this premise. The school had already encouraged girls to study woodwork and metalwork. Now I wanted commercial subjects to be taken by boys.

Fortunately, knowing my ideas for a quick expansion of the department, the Head had set about advertising for staff and the part-time office skills teachers were replaced and a newly qualified graduate employed full-time.

I set about adding new subjects to the departmental curriculum — social economics and accounts to be studied to CSE or "O" level depending on students' progress over the two year course. The ever-popular typewriting and office practice were retained but with emphasis on external examination preparation, mainly for CSE but also for the various levels of Pitman and Royal Society of Arts examinations. I wanted to ensure that pupils either left school at sixteen with a good spread of marketable qualifications or had received ideal preparation for future study at "O" and "A" level in the sixth form.

Over the next few years, I began to achieve most of my goals for the department. The popularity and success achieved with social economics meant that the department was, eventually, able to offer economics, accountancy and sociology to "A" level. The appointment of graduate teachers ensured I had good staffing for these advanced level subjects whilst full and part-time skills teachers assisted me with developing the office skills subjects.

However, I had to remember that I had set out to accept pupils from the full ability range. This meant I had also to cater for the less-able and less-motivated students, often classed as non-exam pupils.

It must be remembered that this was a pretty tough school. My department had to teach a large number of the non-exam pupils and designing courses which might stimulate them was infinitely more demanding than organizing the "O" and "A" level examination courses.

One class of these less-motivated pupils consisted mainly of boys. I decided I would design a two-year course for them entitled "Money Management". Firstly, the course would teach them about wages and salaries, income tax, national insurance and the general mysteries of the first pay packet. I concluded that they would, at some future date, probably need to apply for credit in order to purchase their first motorbike or car or even a mortgage for a house. All this would be covered in the course which would be delivered at a low but interesting level. It couldn't fail.

How wrong can one be? I had every confidence in the necessity of such a course but the pupils, being thoroughly disillusioned by school, particularly so near to their leaving date, had no intention of co-operating. Each lesson was a battle to keep order in the class and achieve some evidence of work having been undertaken. I tried all methods of getting their interest — group work, visits outside school, projects — nothing seemed to work.

At this time, my department was beginning to get a name for itself, with the local education authority, as a school which was expanding the area of business education and achieving excellent results. Because of this, I was often asked to have a student teacher in the department for his/her teaching practice. One such trainee teacher was a mature student. He was an ex-policeman, familiar with outer London boroughs and teenage problems from his career in the police force.

I asked if he would like a challenge. His reply was, "Certainly. I'm here to learn. I need to be familiar with the types of pupils taking commercial subjects at all levels. You've been good enough to give me some examination classes, so I would welcome the opportunity to cover this innovative non-examination "Money Management" class."

He prepared his lessons meticulously and had some good ideas for keeping the students, particularly the boys, interested. He encountered the usual problems of refusal to do any work, excessive noise in the classroom, inability to keep pupils seated, but he battled on.

At the end of one lesson, I found him talking very quietly to a particularly troublesome boy. The whole class had finished their work and were waiting for the end of lesson bell. But the trainee teacher had taken this one boy aside and was talking very quietly to him.

When the class had been dismissed I enquired, "What were you talking to Liam about. He's usually the one causing all the problems."

"That was just it. I've had it up to here with that lad. He refuses to work. He is noisy and disruptive. I'm afraid I came on a bit hard. I took him aside and quietly informed him that if I had any more trouble from him, I would knock him into next week. My policeman-like stance and gruff, but quiet, persistent voice, may have done the trick. I went on to explain my police background and the fact that he was not the first "tearaway" I had dealt with." He finished with, "Let's hope it works."

Reminding him that he would be ill-advised to carry out the promised punishment, I wished him well with the words, "Here's hoping."

Needless-to-say, he had no further trouble with that particular lad nor, indeed with the whole class. However, the reports he had to write for his tutor following these "Money Management" lessons went as follows:

17.1.76

Not easy to evaluate — not very bright class combined with noisy aircraft, the school being situated close to Heathrow airport. Required firm handling.

One or two of the group seem resentful and deliberately inattentive — no overt hostility but manifestly bored with the subject. Some improvement when pointed out to them individually that money, per se, was their concern — demonstrated by question and answer session (the answers had to be dragged out) what could they do with their wages etc?

They are not so dull as they make out — a few really rather bright. I feel I could lick them into shape given the opportunity. They are careless with their paperwork. It was a good idea having them create a signature, exchange it with neighbour and try to forge. Some enthusiasm here — embryonic forgers??

21.1.76

Two girls in this class are daft clowns and disrupt the rest. Loud, vain and empty headed conceit in silly children is tiresome. They both exhibit all the classic symptoms of spoilt brats and required a very firm handling to maintain some semblance of order. Evidently I have here inherited a "difficult" class. I controlled them but it was like sitting on the lid of a boiling kettle — although not as hot, just boring. However, how much learning goes on in this situation? Not much for the rest of the class.

This subject is, unavoidably, not very interesting to children whose minds cannot rise above the level of the Bingo Hall. The principles of banking are utterly beyond their comprehension. Despite reducing the subject to the simplest forms — explanations in monosyllables in a loud clear voice (in order to rise above the aircraft noise and Act II of the resident circus) we are not progressing far at all. And this is a sheer waste of time!

These children are leaving school shortly and undoubtedly most of them have switched off, possibly they were never switched on. It is plain that they (not all, thank God) resent school and resent discipline and are determined not to learn. The few remaining suffer.

I will tidy up banking in the next lesson. Providing I can plant a seed, something may grow, although I imagine, in quite a few cases, the seed will wither away through loneliness. Then I will try to find something which interests them about money management, but what? Wages? Hire Purchase?

One boy claims to have money invested in a building society. Maybe I could use that to introduce house purchase although he was the cause of raucous and sarcastic merriment over his middle class aspirations.

And yet they have such high flown ambitions — air hostess, police-woman, businessman, butcher, bricklayer. The largest, noisiest, commonest and most aggressive girl intends to be a SRN! Her language alone will frighten her patients into a relapse. Her lack of empathy or plain common sense makes her ambition pathetic. In the cold cruel world this lot are in for a rude awakening — they believe the world owes them a living.

23.1.76

Today much better — we managed some work!

By relating it to their impending employment (should they be so lucky) and the high incidence of wage snatches etc, we agreed that wages could be paid into a bank. That got them! I attacked their pockets and they listened. After that it was easy — we covered a good deal of work with cheques and current accounts to the point where notes were taken, no less!!

What a task! I thought, on leaving the police force, I had finished with the awkward, bloody-minded squad. I'll manage them because I'm bigger but what of some young female student or teacher?

Margaret, their usual teacher, is brilliant, but teachers like her must be few and far between — teachers who are prepared to lean on trouble-makers and not worry about popularity (just like a policeman). They learn under her and, by God, they would learn under me!

28.1.76

This is really a dreadful class to try and teach. I'm highly amused at their antics (not that I show it, of course). My role is like that of a lion tamer, standing there cracking a whip and hoping that they will recognise the hoop.

I find that I am reduced to sheer domination and this appears to work. At regular intervals I explode spectacularly and we have a short interval of respect when they call me "Sir".

In these intervals of lucidity we progress a short step further and I manage to penetrate their thick skulls for an instant. Yet, despite all this, I quite like the brats.

30.1.76

I'm getting through to them! Like ploughing blindfold through a mixture of engine oil and treacle, but we seem to be achieving results of sorts.

Already one boy is seriously doubting the wisdom of buying his next motor bike on Hire Purchase because, today, we covered compound interest.

Naturally we had the regular comedian cross-talk but some of the children actually told others to "belt up — he's talking sense." How ridiculous that this should give a feeling of triumph on my part.

Fingers crossed for the future. Fortunately I know that this group are not typical of all fifth year school leavers. If they were, then teaching and I would bid each other a fond adieu.

4.2.76

We eventually finished banking. With the few stalwarts who attend reasonably regularly we will now cover deductions from wages — income tax, national insurance and other "stoppages". Next lesson I may attempt a test.

6.2.76

The test was taken by the nine pupils present today.

The idiots failed miserably and were suitably chastised but one or two did very well. On balance, not a bad performance but, as to its value overall, I remain sceptical. It does appear that my steamroller tactics have proved beneficial.

11.2.76

This class is, quite frankly, boring!

One or two are attentive and bright. The majority are exactly the opposite. Their inattentiveness manifests itself in cretinous din.

I control them by cracking the whip and, for a moment, quietude reigns to re-emerge at the next obscenity when, once again, I lean on them. I have them shifting their seats like some macabre game of musical chairs to the point whereby I point my finger, they sigh heavily and move to another desk, just like trained seals, and I drone on.

We had tears from one girl today, a silly hysteric who waved around a phial of barbiturates, about 100 tablets. Some parents must be "barmy" to allow their children such latitude. We had words, she calmed down. The authorities here will be informed of the potential danger.

More wet nursing than teaching and I don't suffer fools well.

Today we made folders of our work — and this is a class of 15 year olds! Just like dozy infants. God help us. How do they get into this state? The teachers deserve better.

As anticipated, this trainee teacher went on to successfully complete his teacher training course and spent several successful years in his second career.

It should be pointed out that this was not the only non-examination group. In each subject area of the department — economics, accounts, commerce, office skills — I had sufficient pupils to have at least two classes, one aiming for external examinations and the other catering for the non-exam pupils.

Many of the pupils in the non-examination classes were there simply because they refused to work and were disruptive. Warnings that bad behaviour and inattention in class, resulting in lack of progress, would result in them not being entered for any external examinations prior to leaving school met with little concern until the actual examination entries had to be made and parents saw, often for the first time, the consequences of their off-springs' indiscipline. It was at this stage that parents often made demands of the Head that such pupils should be entered. In each case the Head would contact me and, if I could prove that the pupil was unlikely to gain any pass, even at the lowest grade, I was always supported.

Sadly, towards the end of the century, government pressure on schools to enter all pupils for external examinations if they had studied a subject meant there was a general lowering of standards in these external examinations or "dumbing down", as it came to be known.

The battle, in these non-exam classes, was not only with the pupils' boredom and indignation at having to remain at school until the age of sixteen when all they wanted was to start work, but with poor literacy found in such pupils.

Here is an example of a piece of work from a pupil in the non-exam commerce group. Errors are in bold:

The meaning of production

Production is d*evi*ded into three **mane catagories** industry, commerce and Direct services. ✓ Industry is **consernd** with **macking** and assember~~l~~ing the raw goods so they can be **parst** on to the **cermmrce** side and from the commerce side to the ~~Diret~~ direct services side.**X**

The difference between industry and comerce

The difference between industry and **comerce** is that industry deals with raw materials, and **terns** the raw **materiat** into a *finsed* product. Whereas the **comerce** side has the fi<u>nise</u>d product and distributes **ho**to **?** who or what *requiers* them.

By *sluding comerce* we learn about the things around us *lick* the *things* we *by* and how *thay* get to *there* final *desternation* and why prices go up and and how the *government* works.

CHAPTER
SEVEN

Thieving Rogues

As I have mentioned, the Head of this school was a real gentleman. I believe he had been an army officer during the war and became one of the many mature students to undergo a one year teacher training course on his discharge. Although an extremely congenial man to his staff, he could take an aggressive stance with wayward pupils — as I had observed on my first day at the school.

He was supported by two deputy heads. One was a lady who had previously held a post of responsibility at a local girls' school and who had been evacuated with her charges during the war. She was respected by the girls but seemed somewhat out of her depth when confronted by recalcitrant boys.

The other deputy head was a middle-aged man whose non-teaching post was designated head of pastoral care. He was a good-looking, mature gentleman who saw the good side of the most obnoxious pupil. He had acquired two traits. One was that, if the Local Education Authority had any really ill-disciplined pupils who had been expelled from another school they could be assured that this gentleman would accept them with open arms at our school. Maybe this was because he knew he would never have to teach the miscreant.

The other trait, welcomed by the pupils, was that if a badly behaved pupil was referred to him, he or she would often be welcomed with the words, "Sit down. Have a cup of tea and tell me all about it."

This gave the pupil the opportunity to put his/her side of the story, uninterrupted, usually ending with, "That teacher just doesn't understand me."

"I know just what you mean; I often feel the same," would be the sympathetic reply.

With this senior staff set up there was little support for teachers who were having trouble disciplining their classes. Occasionally they could ask for assistance from heads of houses but these stalwarts were usually overloaded with heavy teaching timetables so were seldom available to tackle such incidents.

In my department, I made it clear that the first port of call in the storm of classroom indiscipline was to be me. Fortunately I had been able to ensure appointed staff were, for the most part, excellent disciplinarians. However, inevitably, there were times when disruptive pupils were sent to me so that the class teacher could continue to teach effectively.

I understand that such pupils were somewhat in fear of me. I don't know why except that my previous acting career had enabled me to use facial expressions, timing and gestures which convinced them I meant business. In such circumstances, the pupil would remain in my class until the end of the lesson when I would interview the pupil and teacher together, in the same manner as the Head had dealt with the ring leaders of my first lesson in the school.

The interview would end with my totally supporting the staff, showing mock horror at the misdemeanour reported and warning of the dire consequences which would result from a repeat of such behaviour

On dismissal of the pupil, sometimes near to tears, the staff and I would congratulate ourselves on the outcome and often laugh at our apparent ease of success. Several times staff remarked, "How do you do it? I've never seen her so repentant and close to tears."

My reply could only be, "Bluff!"

I wasn't always successful. One pupil threatened me with, "Just you wait. I'll smack you one outside the school gates."

Fortunately the threat was never carried out, maybe because I showed no fear to the pupil. Sufficient to say that, should it have happened, I know I would have had the backing of the Head and my union. However, I did mention the incident to the senior mistress. Her response was, "She's weird, that one. You know she carries a carving knife and rat poison in her bag?"

Had I known this, I might not have dismissed the threat so readily.

As was the case in most comprehensive schools, at the end of the third year, pupils had to choose which subjects to study for the final two years in preparation for external examinations. Subject teachers were given lists of pupils who had chosen their subjects, but the first lesson was often somewhat confusing if the listed pupils did not arrive.

I reported one such missing pupil to the non-teaching, male deputy head. He commented, "Christ! I've just chucked her into biology."

"But she is on the typing option list," I insisted.

"She's also on the chemistry list," he explained.

Chasing pupils missing from class was also a job for this deputy head. He spent many hours of the day stalking the corridors rounding up absentees and pointing them in the direction of their timetabled lessons. When I asked him to look for yet another missing pupil, his reply was, "Where's that b . . . gone now?"

In the end I became quite amused at his capers. He was usually successful in locating said pupil and escorting them to the correct class — often to the frustration of the teacher who had been enjoying a trouble-free lesson until then.

Unfortunately, there were some incidences of violence against staff. A teacher of French was hit over the head and received a black eye. Another rather weak male teacher was attacked in the corridor by a group of boys and badly kicked in the back.

Most of my encounters with threatening behaviour were at times when I was doing duty during breaks or before and after school. On such occasions one was given an area to supervise. With over 1200 pupils in the school it was difficult to know all the troublemakers and trying to get names from recalcitrant pupils was a nightmare.

I caught one fifth form boy bullying a first year lad in the dinner queue. I asked him to stop only to be given a load of abuse. Attempting to drag him off the boy, I kicked him in the shins, losing my shoe in the attempt. Fortunately, the boy hobbled away, laughing at my antics as I tried to retrieve my shoe by hopping across the muddy path. However, I did report the incident to the Head, fearing I might be accused of assault. The boy knew better, and I heard nothing from him.

Whilst trying to keep another boy from using the drinks machine which had been declared out-of-bounds since it was frequently vandalised and all the money stolen, I was threatened with, "You drive that small green car, don't you? Well, consider this . . . scratches to the paint work are very expensive to repair."

I was not unduly worried but took advice from my ex-policeman trainee teacher. His reply was, "Don't worry. Now that you have this threat on record, any damage to your car can be laid at his door and he, or his parents, will have to pay."

Needless-to-say, the threat was not carried out.

I was on playground duty one morning accompanied by the PE teacher, a tall, fit young man. The playground was invaded by some boys who had left the school at the end of the previous term. They started by just talking to their "mates" but it soon became evident that fighting was about to break out. My male colleague, attempting to escort one of the intruders from the premises was punched by him. I immediately went to my colleague's aid, standing between the burly intruder and being towered over by the 6ft tall PE teacher. I don't know how or why, but the fight ceased and the intruders eventually left. The PE teacher thanked me, and we both reported the incident to the Head. His comment was, "Well, done. But, promise me, you won't ever take that stance again."

On reflection, I agreed it was not my wisest judgement but, given a similar incident, I guess I would, once again, react instinctively.

Another incident of break duty involved the girls' toilets. I found the outside door to the block difficult to open. On eventually gaining entry, I perceived a building full of smoke and a crowd of some twenty girls scuttling into individual cubicles. Knowing that I had infiltrated a smoking den, I demanded that the girls come out and accused them of smoking. The ringleader, a most belligerent girl who was in one of my teaching groups, said, "I weren't smoking."

"You were all smoking," I observed, "considering the amount of smoke still in the air".

"No I weren't, and you can't prove it. I weren't smoking, were I?" she asked of her friends.

A chorus of supporting denial was forthcoming from the rest of the group, obviously frightened of this bully.

I was reporting the incident in the staff room, when another member of staff remarked of the girl, "Julie is the most "mouthy" girl I have ever come across. She is so rude to me. I just keep out of her way while she's in a "mouthy" mood. I'm frightened I might do her an injury otherwise."

As is common practice in all schools, in the case of an absent teacher, a colleague who has a free period is sent to supervise the class of the absentee. I used to dread this "staff cover". I could control my own classes, even my whole department, but I found that standards of discipline in other departments left something to be desired.

I was sent, on one occasion, to supervise the English class of an absent teacher who was noted for his inability to control his classes. I split up the noisy groups, moving several boys to different desks. I gave out the set work and hoped to get on with some marking. The boys began to make rude noises. Warnings, threats, pleas, were all lost on them, and the noise escalated.

Added to this, the teacher in the next room was attempting to teach with the door open. Shouts of, "Put that chair down", "Write about the damned thing", etc. etc. were met by giggles and then screams of delight from the unruly pupils. Chaos reigned in the class and was igniting insubordination within surrounding classes, including the one I was supervising.

I had had enough of this use of what was supposed to be one of my free periods, so I took my chair outside the class and continued to do my marking in the corridor.

The head of department came along the corridor. "Anything wrong?" she enquired.

"Not really. It's just that the boys are intent upon making rude noises and generally being objectionable.

I'm not prepared to be abused, so will control the class from out here."

"Oh, I see. Well, I've got a class waiting for me," was her reply, and off she went, passing for a second time the chaotic class next door without so much as a sideways glance. I was amazed. She was supposed to be in charge of the department. No wonder my staff were always saying how supportive I was to them. Clearly not all heads of department took their responsibilities so earnestly.

Next on the scene was a deputy head. I waited for her to reach the spot where I was sitting marking and enquire why I was outside the classroom. She didn't get that far. The teacher in the rioting classroom asked her to come in and restore order for him. She spent a few minutes inside talking to the class, with the door shut. Then she and the class teacher emerged into the corridor, he thanking her for her help and the class returning to the same level of noise and chaos as before her interception. Again she glanced at me but went away without question.

I learned one lesson from supervising this English class: if there were too many troublemakers to put outside the room, go outside yourself. It was obviously not disapproved of by senior staff!

I was just pleased that I appeared to be able to keep discipline within my own department. Periods of break duty and cover for absent staff were only minor parts of what was usually a pleasant working day.

Another incident, when I was sent to cover the class of an absent teacher, shows the differing attitudes of staff towards classroom organisation and control. The head of the mathematics department had decided to follow a new system of teaching maths which involved students working in groups on a variety of topics. As each topic was successfully completed the group moved to a more taxing topic for which the teacher was able to give any individual tuition. In theory, the method worked well and seemed to be welcomed by the pupils. However, supervision of such a "noisy" classroom was quite alien to me. Some groups were working on statistics which involved much throwing of dice, most of which seemed to land on neighbouring desks or the floor. Other groups were conducting surveys of pupils' opinions, others needed to use mathematical instruments not readily available in each pupil's pencil case. I could not understand why so many pupils had to "borrow" rulers rather than bring their own essential equipment to such a lesson.

I entered the classroom and restored enough order to point out that I understood they were capable of continuing with the group work as normal. I enquired if any needed my help, although what help I could be in a subject so alien to me was seriously in question. I explained, "Now that you are all in the correct groups, know what you are doing, and have the requisite equipment, I presume you are capable of working on your own whilst I continue with my marking. After all, this is supposed to be my free period."

Within minutes, I had queues of children at my desk requesting information, equipment and, worst of all, my help. The noise level was rising, and my nerves were becoming frayed. I again approached the class, "It's no good asking for my help. I am not a maths teacher," I explained. "If you can't manage the work you are doing, choose another topic card and work quietly on that."

I might as well have saved my breath. The noise level rose and rose. Complaints from me were met with cries of, "We have to talk because we are working together."

When one group talks loudly, the next group needs to shout, and the next group to shout louder. To me this was a logical outcome of organizing teaching by this method — a method I could never implement.

As a last resort I stuffed cotton wool into my ears and sat at the desk doing my marking, quite oblivious to the commotion around me. When a pupil approached my desk to ask a question there would be a chorus from the rest of the class, "She can't hear you. She's got cotton wool stuffed in her ears."

It worked. The lesson passed relatively peacefully; I did a lot of marking. How much maths work was done I hate to think but, in this school, it was evident that the teacher's sanity was of paramount importance, and I intended to remain sane enough to do my job and ensure the success of my own department.

It was not just that this was a tough school. The whole area was known to the police.

The school went through a spate of break-ins and fires, mostly during the weekends. One had one's suspicions as to which pupils might be involved but, inevitably, it was whole families (of which past-pupils were members) who were behind many of the local criminal activities.

The presence of police cars at the front of the school on a Monday morning was a relatively common sight and heralded yet another break-in or minor arson attack during the weekend. But the Head was reluctant to blame our own pupils for such criminal activities although evidence certainly pointed to them. One such incident involved a box of chocolates.

It was the Head's custom, at Christmas time, to purchase several boxes of chocolates to give to members of his office staff. On this occasion, having purchased them with his usual care, he had them locked away in the stationery cupboard next to his study, awaiting the end of term.

A few days later we had a break-in. Usually, the thieves helped themselves to the more "marketable" items such as typewriters, video recorders or portable television sets. This time, the school office was broken into. The safe, containing quite a large sum of money, was taken, and a great deal of mess was made. Filing cabinets were rifled and pupil records strewn over the floor. For some strange reason, the stationery cupboard was also entered, though nobody could guess why anyone, even a pupil, would want to steal stationery supplies. In fact, apart from evidence of a search taking place, nothing seemed to be missing.

It was a little coincidental that two pupils, members of one family, turned up at school a few days later in brand new sheepskin coats. The staff, as a whole, persuaded the Head that he should have a quiet word with these two boys in an endeavour to establish where they had got their coats.

Reluctantly, the Head undertook the interview and was pleased to be able to report to the staff that it was "quite alright." The boys explained that their father had just won the football pools and had been generous with his winnings.

The Head congratulated the boys on the family's good fortune and almost apologized for doubting that the said coats had been acquired other than honestly. Needless-to-say there were those among the staff who were not so readily convinced.

On the last day of term, the sister of the two boys in question knocked on the Head's door and presented him with a Christmas present — a gorgeous box of chocolates. They were, she pointed out, a tribute to a Head who was respected for his fairness and support for his pupils.

It was not until the end of the day, when the Head went to the stationery cupboard to get the presents he had carefully chosen for his office staff, that he had doubts about the genuineness of the girl. The largest and most attractive box, the gift chosen for his secretary, had mysteriously disappeared. Even he was a little confused when he realized that the unsolicited gift had been identical to the one he had chosen for his secretary. But, as he said, "There's a lot of these boxes on sale at this time of the year, and certainly there is no proof that this is the box which has been mislaid."

On another school day, one of the suspects from the recent break-in was caught mid-afternoon walking along the corridor with something concealed under his jumper. The said object turned out to be a cash box full of money. On closer inspection, it was evident that it had recently been removed from the vandalized drinks machine.

Fortunately (or rather unfortunately for the criminals), the same boys were later caught by the police breaking and entering a local house. In the course of interrogation, they admitted to the recent break-in at the school among other offences.

CHAPTER
EIGHT

Communications

With so many pupils and such a large staff, communications were of vital importance but one had to be discreet in their use.

Early morning briefings, monthly full staff meetings and Heads of Departments meetings were all times when the senior staff could impart essential information, but it was left to Heads of Departments and Heads of Houses to hold relevant staff meetings to discuss matters of immediate concern or to implement new principles.

For my part, members of my department knew that I was always available to offer advice or assistance when they were having problems, particularly of disciplining classes. When I held departmental meetings, usually every half term, I always circulated a written agenda and confirmed decisions made by means of a written memo. My idea was to "cover my back" and ensure that I could always refer to the written communication should the matter not be dealt with as anticipated.

Indeed, I became quite famous for my memos. I lost count of the number sent to the Head and other senior staff, reporting incidents of indiscipline encountered whilst doing various duties around the school. I was always supported by the Head and, on one occasion, by my union.

It was obvious that the school attracted a large number of undesirable pupils. This was not only because of the local environment, or "catchment area", but also because the non-teaching Deputy Head would never refuse to accept a troublemaker excluded by some other school when the Local Education Authority was at a loss as to where to place the expelled pupil. On one occasion, the Union became involved when the Head agreed to expel a troublesome pupil who had been particularly rude to me, only to readmit the pupil on the advice of the Local Education Authority. Suffice to say that the result was that I was not expected to teach this pupil nor come into contact with her during the rest of her days at the school.

On one occasion, during a free period, I toured the school trying to locate pupils who should be in one of my department's lessons but who were obviously refusing to attend. I found a girl and told her to report to her lesson. She was reluctant to do so, but I insisted on escorting her to the correct classroom. Walking closely behind her, I accidentally trod on the back of her shoe. Her reaction was to turn round and punch me in the stomach. Needless-to-say I was furious and in no mood to accept such behaviour.

I demanded to see the Head, who was in conference with local dignitaries at the time. Efforts on the part of the Senior Mistress to placate me were useless so, being near the end of the day, she advised me to leave the school and calm down before returning to have the incident investigated. I did just this but, before returning to school the next day, I visited my doctor to ascertain any injuries sustained. His response was, "I think the hurt has been more to your pride than anything else. Yes, there is a little tenderness there but no real injury."

I was still not in the best of moods when I eventually got to school and announced that I would sue for industrial injury.

Several members of the senior staff tried to persuade me against such a course of action, referring to adverse publicity for the school which might result from such a course of action. But my mind was made up. In the end, I had to go before a medical panel appointed by the Local Education Authority, and I was awarded the princely sum of £92 for my "injury". The school received no adverse publicity. Only the staff knew of my compensation.

Had more staff gone to the same lengths to report on their injuries, maybe something would have been done to create an environment of better discipline in the school.

Another incident involved a black pupil. She was quite an intelligent girl who was underachieving in my subjects. One day, when she refused to answer a question in class, I unconcernedly enquired,

"Did you understand the question? Or do you have problems with the English language?"

The girl took exception to my query and reported to the Head that I was being racially discriminating since she had been born and bred in England. Her parents came up to the school and suggested that they would report the incident to the local Race Relations Department.

Not being at all perplexed by this threat, I decided to go myself to seek advice from this local authority department. Several members of staff pleaded with me not to do so.

"Just think of the adverse publicity for the school," they warned. "You have no idea what the outcome will be. You will find it very difficult to put your point of view to this department. You are in for a rough ride."

Such warnings did not deter me, and I went, the next day, to visit the offices of the local Race Relations Department. The person in charge was a black man. He listened carefully to my report of the incident and my confession that, perhaps, I should have been more aware of the pupil's personal file, which may have shown that she was, in fact, born in this country. His verdict somewhat surprised me.

"Well, I must admit that I usually have to defend black people who have been racially discriminated against. It will be my pleasure to support you, a white person, should any question of guilt be pointed at you by this black family."

I felt totally vindicated and was pleased to report the outcome to the staff at the school. The only point scored by the family in this incident was that they refused to have their daughter taught by me for the rest of her time in the school. With a large departmental staff it was easy to transfer her to another group, and she went on to do well in her external examinations.

The next year her sister joined the department. The parents expected her to receive the best tuition, presumably being taught by the Head of Department, but I was able to reason that, "Surely you would not want her to be taught by a perceived racist."

She was summarily demoted to the second set, taught by another member of staff.

Communication between me and one other member of my department, who taught in the next classroom, took on a somewhat unusual method. This other teacher had spent some time teaching in a Young Offenders' Institute and had picked up a few tips from her students there. Apparently messages could be tapped out along the central heating pipes.

Being rather an old building, the heating in the school was by means of radiators and pipes running around and between the classrooms. We decided to adopt this somewhat unusual method of communication. If the teacher needed to speak to me on a matter of urgency she would simply tap twice on the pipes, and we would meet in the corridor outside the classrooms to converse.

I was fortunate in having a very supportive Head of Faculty. He was an extremely experienced teacher of mathematics who was adored by his pupils. To enter his class whilst he was teaching was a lesson in how to keep discipline. His pupils always worked in silence yet he had an easy rapport with them and had schooled them to play a joke on any visitor to his lesson. Whilst talking to the visitor he would raise his hand slightly and the whole class would rise silently and remain standing until another flick of the hand instructed them to sit and continue work. I must admit that most visitors soon became aware of the joke but played along with the teacher for the sake of the pupils.

I learned a lot from this Head of Faculty. He was extremely supportive of me and of my department and was very astute in dealing with inter-departmental problems. Many a time he had to pour oil on the troubled waters as my hot-headedness lead me into conflicts with senior staff, departmental heads or other staff members.

He had just one annoying habit. He spoke in abbreviations, using initial letters for certain phrases. He once informed me that he had met the PA to the MD of RTZ. For the most part I was able to understand him but I must admit to the occasional mumbled acceptance of his topic of conversation when I had no idea what he was talking about.

The heating of the school was another cause for concern. The teaching rooms allocated to my department were, unfortunately, situated at the end of the heating route. Hence, they were the last to receive the central heating and were often very cold in the winter. Pupils got used to the fact that they needed to bring their coats to lessons in my department and even became adept at typing whilst wearing gloves.

On one occasion, I was teaching Health and Safety at Work as part of the office practice syllabus. The pupils enquired what the minimum working temperature was deemed to be according to the Act. When I told them they immediately demanded a thermometer be placed in each room along the corridor in which we had our classes.

With a little co-operation from the Science department, I acceded to their request, and we were soon able to record temperatures well below the minimum permitted by the Act. On one occasion a group of students were given permission to approach the Head with the temperature chart compiled over the past week and demand either that supplementary heating be provided or they would refuse to attend lessons in those rooms.

I hate to admit it, but these pupils did more to solve the problem of cold classrooms than I and my colleagues had done. Several electric heaters were provided and the topic of conversation in the staffroom was often that of the temperature in the coldest classrooms of the school. For some time, at each morning staff briefing, I would relay the temperatures of each room in my department and, where not of an acceptable level, await the Senior staff's allocation of alternative teaching rooms.

One of the most acute interruptions to communication was the noise of aircraft taking off and landing at the nearby London Heathrow Airport. When a plane passed overhead it was often impossible to continue to speak. On my first day in the school I had thought that this would result in the students "switching off" in the middle of a lesson but, to my amazement, as the plane passed, I stopped talking (often mid-sentence) and merely continued when it had passed. The pupils did just the same. I guess, as most lived nearby, they were used to enduring this noisy interruption throughout their lives.

The school was a relatively old building and certainly not double glazed. I taught at the school for over fifteen years. During all this time we tried to get double glazing installed without success. The problem was even more acute during the period of external examinations. The Examination Boards had to be alerted to the fact that, should a certain runway be used on the day of oral examinations, it would be necessary to re-timetable the tests. This was particularly important when pupils were taking music examinations which involved listening to notes or when my pupils were taking shorthand examinations.

This phenomenon became even more acute during the time Concorde was in operation. When that plane took off, using a certain runway, the building seemed to vibrate.

Timetabling in a large comprehensive school is a nightmare. It is usually left to one of the Deputy Heads who spends endless hours during the summer term trying to accede to the wishes of each Head of Department for the correct allocation of teaching periods for his/her subjects and the allocation of the correct staff.

Fortunately, in a Business Studies department most staff are multi-qualified and can teach most of the subjects offered. Not all staff could teach the office skills, but such teachers were not usually in short supply. The other teachers could usually teach a variety of subjects from economics, commerce, accountancy and, when it was eventually introduced into the department, sociology. The competency of such teachers meant, however, that some were more able than others to teach the "A" level courses. I fought hard to ensure the staffing of my department was just as I and my staff requested. All our subjects were popular options and classes were often quite large, compared to some other subjects. I could well have ensured each of my staff being gainfully employed for all 40 periods of the week but the staff in charge of timetabling always liked each teacher to have one or two free periods which, although classed as marking or preparation periods, were usually times when they could be called upon to cover a lesson for an absent member of staff.

Not all departments were staffed so competently. In some cases a department suffered from too few pupils opting for their subject in the final years of schooling, so that the members of staff of the department had more than a fair share of free periods and were quickly coerced into teaching other subjects, regardless of their ability so to do.

One Deputy Head, who undertook the timetabling, had little respect for staff specialisms. One year the Head of Religious Education was timetabled to teach French. Her plea, "I can't speak the language" was no reason for her to refuse the task.

When the Head of History was told she would have to teach modern languages she was asked, "Which would you prefer to teach, French or German?"

Her reply was, "Neither, they're both Greek to me."

How fortunate I was to have such a multi-talented staff and a supportive Head of Faculty at this crucial time of the year.

CHAPTER
NINE

The External Examiner

Writing as I do in the early part of the twenty-first century, it is difficult to explain the period in which I taught, and examined commercial subjects, including the office skills.

In the 1950s, pupils who opted for commercial studies were taught touch typewriting on manual machines. Not until the 1970s and early 80s were electric and later electronic typewriters introduced into schools and colleges. Of course in the late 1980s, computer studies and word processing surpassed the typewriting lessons.

During a long and varied career in teaching typewriting, I had successfully taught visually impaired and disabled young people. Two of my fourteen- to sixteen-year-old pupils in a comprehensive school were one-handed typists for whom I devised a special keyboard mastery system so that they were able to become as efficient touch typists as their able-bodied classmates. They achieved success in external typewriting examinations without application of any dispensations or special considerations.

In the era of manual typewriters, great skill was needed in the use of special erasers should typographical errors have to be corrected. Before the emergence of the photocopier, the typist was responsible for making copies of documents by the use of carbon paper or by means of ink or spirit duplicators for which stencils or masters must first be produced. In all these cases, the accuracy of the original typewritten document was essential if time was to be saved in making difficult corrections of multiple copies.

Typists were responsible for the attractive appearance of their work and many simple mathematical calculations were needed to centrally place work both vertically and horizontally on the page.

In the case of tables of figures, ruling in red ink was included to add ease of reading and attractiveness to the display. Many a time-consuming and carefully typewritten piece of tabulation was spoilt when the typist had to rule lines with a pen and ink, blotting each line carefully to prevent smudges.

Accuracy was important, not only because correcting errors was time consuming and an art in itself, but because employers insisted on very high standards. For instance, a typist employed in a solicitor's office was not allowed to correct a typographical error on a legal document. It was maintained that erasing an error could be seen as an attempt to forge the document. If a typist made a mistake whilst typing a legal document she merely started afresh.

It was amid this atmosphere of high standards of accuracy that I became interested in external examining.

I first worked as an assistant examiner (marker) of typewriting for Pitman Examinations Institute in 1960. Later I acted in a similar fashion for Royal Society of Arts Examinations marking their Secretarial Duties examinations.

As my interests broadened and my career developed, I taught more and more commercial subjects — bookkeeping and accounts, commerce, economics and later business studies, all of which I went on to examine in various capacities until 2005 when, at the age of 75 years, I was forced to retire from most of the examining boards.

In 1970, apart from examining typewriting and secretarial duties, I undertook the marking of "O" level commerce for one of the major examining boards.

But great changes were on their way. With the widening of the teaching curriculum in the secondary and, later, the comprehensive schools, it was evident that the external examinations system needed an overhaul.

In the first half of the twentieth century, some eight university boards offered matriculation through School Certificate examinations, usually taken after five years of study at a grammar school. These required a candidate to pass in a group of subjects. A Higher Schools Certificate could be taken in two or four subjects that had been studied at a higher level from 16 to 18 years.

In 1951, the General Certificate of Education was introduced and offered examination at Ordinary ("O") and Advanced ("A") level. Unlike the former Schools Certificate and Higher Schools Certificate, these examinations could be taken in single subjects. The fixing of a lower age limit for the "O" level examination at 16 years avoided the examination being taken by children attending the secondary modern schools who normally left school at fifteen years of age.

The universities' hold over these examinations had been all very well when "O" and "A" levels formed the bench mark for university entrance, but, now, methods of examining the more vocational subjects needed to be developed beyond the few existing boards such as Royal Society of Arts (RSA), Pitman Examination Institute, Faculty of Teachers in Commerce, Union of Lancashire and Cheshire Institutes etc. Added to this, with the raising of the school leaving age and the disappearance of grammar schools in favour of the all-ability comprehensive schools, an examination was needed that would cater for the average and below average students.

It was in this climate that the Certificate of Secondary Education (CSE) was introduced — an examination which would cater for the average and below average sixteen year olds. Previously, it was expected that the academic top twenty-five per cent of the age range would be entered for General Certificate of Education, Ordinary level (GCE "O" level) in each subject studied.

The Beloe Committee, set up by the government in 1958, criticised examining boards for not involving teachers sufficiently in the examination process. The committee recommended the new examination which could be taken by pupils at the end of the fifth year of a secondary course. It was assumed that the top 20 per cent of sixteen year olds would take GCE "O" level in at least four subjects. This would provide evidence of academic success commensurate with further studies and eventual university entrance. The new CSE examination was aimed at the next 20 per cent of sixteen year olds who would take the examination in four subjects and a further 20 per cent who could sit one or more individual subject examinations. It was now obvious that some 60 per cent of all sixteen years olds could look forward to preparing for and sitting examinations at the end of their secondary school course whether in a grammar, secondary modern or comprehensive school.

Following these recommendations, the new examination, the CSE, was introduced in 1963. It was to be a national examination administered by some thirteen regional examining boards. The first examinations were held in 1965.

The new examination gave teachers a unique opportunity to create, for the first time in educational history, an examination system which would be wholly the servant of the schools, reflecting the highest professional standards of the teachers who would run it by having representatives on each of the examining boards.

It was in this climate of teacher involvement that I first became interested in CSE examining. My first set of pupils took the new CSE in typewriting. The examining board used was that of the locality in which the school was based, but the emphasis was on initial teacher marking. All teachers marked to a basic marking scheme and then met together with the moderator and chief examiner at a central venue to establish grade boundaries and uniformity of marking.

This proved to be my first insight into the vagaries of marking. Many teachers had marked their students' work in pencil. A quick glance at such scripts gave a much more favourable impression than those which had been marked in red ink. Added to this, many teachers had missed typographical errors and others had been over pedantic in the application of correct, or acceptable, layouts for typewritten documents.

Although teacher panels and in-service training sessions were set up, few teachers bothered to attend, and some local education authorities were less than generous in allowing expenses and/or time off to attend such meetings.

It was soon evident that the examining boards needed to take more charge of the assessment process. They appointed Chief Examiners to construct the initial question papers, committees, which included teacher representatives, to approve such papers and teams of assistant examiners, led by the Chief Examiner, to mark all candidates' work externally.

This is when I became much more interested and was soon appointed, first as Chief Examiner for an office studies examination, and later for examinations in typewriting and commerce. I worked for two of the major examination boards and enjoyed this initial furore into external examining immensely.

I remember the first commerce CSE paper I wrote for one board. It contained sixty questions. The procedure involved was that my first draft went to a Reviser who commented upon its accuracy and compliance with the syllabus, a second draft went before a panel which consisted of the Board's representatives and representatives of teachers of the subject.

I spent over two weeks diligently preparing my first set of questions and the relevant mark schemes and despatched them to the Reviser for his comments. Within one week, they were returned. Two questions had been accepted. For the other 58, I was advised either to re-write completely or to make minor adjustments. On receipt, I threw the offending package into the corner of my study and prepared to abandon my idea of being a Chief Examiner. Luckily, I had second thoughts and eventually set about revising my work, appreciating the comments of the Reviser. The second draft went before the panel and needed very little further revision.

By 1970, there were thirteen CSE examination boards, and I was working for three of them.

On one occasion, as Chief Examiner of a CSE examination in typewriting and office studies, I was conducting a co-ordination meeting of some fifty assistant examiners prior to their marking of candidates' work. Naturally many of the assistant examiners were teachers who had entered their own pupils for the examination and were keen to gain the maximum number of passes.

My marking scheme had been approved by the examining board's panel at the same time as the question papers, and I saw no reason to amend it, other than marginally. Teachers, who could see their pupils being penalized, possibly for something they had erroneously taught, became vociferous in their demands for amendments, but I stood my ground. There was no way I was going to compromise first-class, well-prepared candidates in favour of less deserving work, even if resulting from poor teaching.

During this hectic meeting, the Board's representative, the Subject Officer, left the room. I found him, later in the day, in his office puffing nervously on a cigarette saying, "Those teachers put the fear of God into me. Have they calmed down yet?"

"Yes," was my reply. "They've all agreed to mark according to my marking scheme, and you can be assured I shall make constant checks throughout the marking period to ensure they all remain co-ordinated."

This seemed to reassure him, and he approached future meetings with more confidence. As for me, I knew I had to be tough and single-minded to hold down the job of a Chief Examiner. I knew I could do it — and enjoy it.

It was not long before the government decided to rationalize external examinations by combing CSE and "O" levels into one common examination to be taken by all sixteen year olds. I was elected to the National Consultative Committee for commercial subjects as the representative of two of the CSE boards for whom I worked. Other members of this committee were drawn from the "O" levels boards and subject experts.

There was a long consultative period, but eventually a new examination was born.

This new examination was called the General Certificate of Secondary Education (GCSE) and it was first examined in 1972. It offered a plethora of subjects, including vocationals. Candidates gaining grades A, B, C (or 1, 2, 3) were deemed to have reached the old "O" level or CSE grade 1 standard. Other grades reflected lower levels of attainment with grades E and F being that of the average sixteen year old and Grade G being the minimum for a "Pass" grade.

The progress of GCSE examinations has been chequered. At first, standards were rigidly maintained and comparison with the old examinations accurate. However, sadly, standards have been allowed to slip until, writing in the early part of the twenty first century, I am ashamed at the low level required to attain high grades in an examination in which few fail, and in which the ability to spell and write grammatically is hardly rewarded. The examination does a disservice to the academically gifted when such large percentages of candidates receive A$\star$ (the top grade) in most subjects.

I fought hard during my latter years of examining to maintain standards. At one grading meeting, at which the committee of examiners, teacher representatives and board personnel met to fix the grade boundaries by looking at the work of candidates in each borderline zone, there was much disagreement as to the lowest percentage acceptable for a grade C (the crucial "O" level equivalent standard). We argued, and re-read candidates' scripts. The board representative worked out statistics to see how great a percentage difference would occur between this and last year's grade C candidates.

Eventually the problem was solved. The board's representative announced, "My stats show you should accept the lower mark."

The reply from the subject experts was, "But, given the scripts before us, such candidates are not up to a grade C."

"If you don't agree the lower figure, you will all have to reconvene in August when most of you will be on your annual holidays."

A quick look at diaries, resulted in an immediate acceptance of the lower mark. No member of the committee was willing to interrupt a summer holiday to repeat the grading process.

Some examining boards exploited the good nature of assistant examiners, refusing to pay attendance allowances for attending meetings.

I attended one such co-ordination of markers. Being new to that particular board, I was expected to arrive one hour prior to the main meeting to undergo training. The meeting itself was scheduled to take place between 10a.m. and 4p.m.

Having spent a boring training hour listening to information I already knew and had implemented for several years, I enquired, "How much are we getting paid for our attendance today."

"Nothing," was the reply. "This board has never paid for attending meetings."

"In that case, count me out. I've got more profitable ways of using my time," I replied.

Being already short of assistant examiners, the board's representative was summoned, and I put my case to her.

"I work for several boards all of which pay an attendance allowance. I do not intend to spend seven hours here without payment."

"Give me a few minutes. I'll get back to you," was her reply.

Within an hour, she approached me and enquired, "Would you accept £30 for the day?"

This being a realistic offer, in fact somewhat above that which I was prepared to accept, I agreed but enquired, "I presume all examiners will be treated in the same way."

A reluctant, "Yes" was forthcoming, and news quickly spread among the examiners who had worked for several years without such payment.

"Guess what," they began to comment, "we're getting paid for today's meeting. Who changed the board's mind?"

Naturally I was popular among my colleagues — at least for that marking session.

I have already mentioned my regret that poor handwriting, spelling, punctuation and grammar were not penalized in the new GCSE examination. Indeed, after some time, examiners were instructed, in general, to ignore such errors and mark only the content of the answer. It was later decided that five per cent of the total available marks would be allocated to "spelling, punctuation and grammar" (spg marks).

Although only a small percentage, this was open to subjectivity. Some examiners felt no candidate was worthy of maximum marks, others that any attempt at a written answer must be worth at least one or two marks. Some chief examiners insisted that candidates who did not gain top grade marks for their question paper answers should not be awarded maximum marks for spg, however well written their answers.

Before I finished marking business studies papers in 2006, this percentage had been reduced to two and examiners and candidates were told which question and answer would be used for this assessment. The result was that many candidates wrote illegibly with poor spelling and punctuation but took special care with just the one identified question when they at least attempted to correct spelling errors — although I remain amazed at the number of candidates unable to spell the word "business" when it formed the title of the question paper!

For some thirty years, I worked as Principal Examiner and Reviser for Cambridge International examinations.

These were rewarding positions since the level of international "O" levels and, latterly International GCSEs, remained high. Considering that candidates were taking examinations written in English, which was invariably their second language, the standard of spelling and grammar, in general, was far above that of candidates to UK GCSE examinations.

When a new syllabus is developed, the examining board arranges a series of teacher training sessions. I was fortunate enough to be sent abroad to conduct some of these. I remember, in Singapore, that the teachers attending the course were very keen to learn the new syllabus and asked many questions to ensure they were well able to present the new content to their students. Many of the teachers who would be teaching the new syllabus for office studies and information technology were not specialists in the area of commercial subjects yet they worked extremely hard to ensure they were aware of the demands of the new syllabus. Indeed, I was impressed by the work ethic in Singapore. As trainers, we were expected to work from 8a.m. until 5p.m. and then to conduct a de-briefing session afterwards. At the end of the two weeks' training, we were all glad to return to England with our somewhat shorter working days.

In Lesotho, the weather one day was so hot that, whilst sitting at my desk supervising assistant examiners, I slipped off my shoes. A representative of the Ministry of Education decided to visit my group unexpectedly and spotted my lack of shoes. I apologized, explained that I was not used to such heat and quickly donned my shoes. His comment was, "Yes, it is hot but — see, I wear shoes and a tie and a suit."

I felt duly admonished and remained correctly attired at all times for the remainder of my visit.

The meetings in Lesotho were conducted in local schools. I visited one classroom with the teacher of an "O" level accounting group. The room was so full of desks there was no room to set them out in rows with space between them. I enquired, "Is this where they store the spare desks?"

"No," was his replay. "This is my classroom."

"But, how do the students get to the back row with no space between the desks?"

"No student enters the room until I arrive, then, those first to enter walk over the desks to fill up the back rows first."

"How many students do you have in your class?" I enquired.

"There are sixty in my "O" level accounts class and about fifty in my commerce class."

"How do you cope with discipline?" I enquired. "Surely it must get rather noisy."

"No," he answered. "I do the talking. The students only answer when questioned. They have no textbooks, so they are kept very busy taking notes."

He went on to explain that pens and paper were also in short supply. Very few students had access to class texts. The teacher had the textbook and taught from that and the chalk board.

Despite this, standards in the external examinations were usually higher than in the UK, and candidates' work was usually well presented with good spelling and punctuation.

However, with English being the candidates' second language some amusing exam howlers were encountered. For instance, a question relating to the security or otherwise of paying by credit card got the following response from one candidate:

"If the card is lost all you money is gone, unless the person who discovers it is stupid or Christian."

Other such howlers included:

"Net profit is profit gained by a business man which he doesn't deserve."

"Consumer protection protects consumers from adultery which might be committed by manufacturers."

"Air transport is used for human kidneys which, if sent by sea, the kidney will get raw."

Candidates in the land-locked countries, particularly in Africa, find the study of sea transport somewhat theoretical.

One candidate explained,

"In the sea there is a lot of water and if goods are heavy the boat will sink."

Another warned,

"There are big animals in the sea which attack the ship."

One wonders just how much connection candidates from third world countries have with banks. One candidate recommended,

"To increase his capital a sole trader should go and see the bank because all the people at the bank are kind people."

So desperate are some overseas candidates to attain a "pass" in an external examination that they write notes to the assistant examiner marking the paper. One such plea went something like this,

"Dear Examiner,

Please, please give me a pass this time. I've worked really hard AND I revised. I know I didn't work hard enough last time but this time is different and I just need to pass."

Another said.

"Please give me a pass this time. I've been working horrimendously hard."

Whilst bribes such as,

"If you pass me I'll always pray for you", or *"I want to be your friend, here is my phone number"*,

never, sadly, included a monetary incentive!

Conversely, UK candidates entered, sometimes reluctantly, for a GCSE examination will spend their time writing mindless drivel, doodling or drawing on the answer booklets. Those whose knowledge is somewhat lacking will often explain, *"Our teacher never taught us this"*, or *"This question is just too difficult."*

One can sympathise with frustrated candidates who claim, *"I've told you the answer already"*, or *"Ask a silly question and you'll get a silly answer."*

Modern examining boards provide booklets in which candidates write their relevant answer beneath the question. The idea is to give candidates some indication as to the length of answer required. A question requiring a short answer may be allocated three lines whilst one requiring an essay-type answer may be allocated a whole page.

One candidate, who had decided to enlighten the examiner to all the knowledge gleaned during her studies, wrote at great length for every answer. Hence, her writing often protruded into the margin or was continued on a separate sheet. At one point she wrote, *"Why don't you give us room to write the answer?"*

Later, she explained, *"I've got big handwriting."*

Finally her frustration exploded with, *"I'm getting p . . . ed off with this."*

I enjoyed my forty years as an external examiner and like to think that it helped to develop my own understanding of my subjects and enabled me to prepare my own students more rigorously for these crucial examinations. Above all, it alerted me to the standards achieved by candidates worldwide and from a variety of educational establishments. My only regret is that I was not able to fight to maintain the high standards of UK GCSE examinations.

It is so sad that our system of external examining for worthwhile qualifications, once the envy of the world, has been allowed to fall to standards which appear to be so relatively low.

CHAPTER TEN

Head Teachers

The Head Teacher can make or break a school but a good school will survive despite its Head.

During over forty years of teaching, I served under several different Head Teachers. Each had his or her own ideas of running a successful school. Sometimes, despite rather than with, the support of the staff. Each had his or her own personality, and, from each, I learned something about education. Most supported my enthusiasm for my specialist subjects and generally appreciated the expertise I brought to my teaching through my work as an external examiner.

I guess the one who first impressed me, not favourably unfortunately, was the Head of one of the grammar schools forced to accept me and my vocational subjects into his "cathedral" of academic excellence. In the grammar school setting, the Head was revered from afar, maintaining a status of awe and splendour as he swept through the assembly hall in his academic gown to be joined, on the platform, with similarly gowned senior staff. When this school was reformed, within the comprehensive system, into a senior high school to which all fourteen year olds could aspire, his presence became less obvious. With growing indiscipline within the school, he retreated to his office leaving the day-to-day running of the school to his deputies.

Such Heads are usually unapproachable by staff or pupils, but I must say that I received a great deal of support from this particular Head when I applied for qualified teacher status. As I have explained, without a degree, albeit with Teachers' diplomas in Shorthand and Typewriting, an ALAM (Eloc) from London Academy of Music and Dramatic Art and membership of professional organisations for commercial teachers, I was still deemed unqualified by the Ministry of Education. To obtain qualified teacher status, I would need to undertake a two-year mature student teacher training course. I was studying for "A" levels through correspondence courses and was allowed to enter the examinations through the school at which I was teaching. I applied, and was accepted, for a two-year teacher training course at Redland College, a part of the University of Bristol. After qualifying, I returned to this school as teacher in charge of commercial subjects within the economics department. Yes, I owed much to that Head and was sorry to leave his school when my family moved to the north west because of my husbands' job.

The next two Heads, both men, were quite different. One had very definite ideas about teaching methods and the curriculum. He insisted on mixed ability teaching in every subject, something which was quite alien to me. He was over-emphatic about staff

91

administration. We were expected to write copious lesson plans and reports and to attend endless meetings. I lasted only six months in that environment. At the next school, the Head was a charming man appreciative of every member of his staff and supportive to both staff and pupils, all of whom adored him.

When I moved back to the south, to the London area, I encountered the Head who was a perfect gentleman — so much so that the pupils (and staff) took advantage of him. He, himself, had been an "emergency-trained" teacher — a scheme offered immediately after the second world war to combat the teacher shortage. Like many of his fellow "emergency-trained" teachers, he had a background in the armed forces which one would have supposed would give him the ability to instil strict discipline among his "troops". Unfortunately, this was not so.

The large staff of this school included several politically left wing activists. They found it easy to take over staff meetings and pressurize this *gentle man* to agree to somewhat bizarre traits. For instance, they insisted that there should be no school uniform. Homework was considered to be of little value and several teachers refused to set it for their pupils. Competition was frowned upon, not only in the classroom but also on the sports field. Needless-to-say, discipline suffered and there were times when I despaired at my ability to control particularly unruly children. I soon learned, however, that it was a case of the survival of the fittest in this large school — a school which gave me the potential to expand my teaching activities and develop a commercial department of which I, and the school, would be proud.

Like many fellow teachers, I set about establishing my own standards of discipline and work ethic. Fortunately, it worked. Whilst the Head was always there for me when I had new ideas or problems, I always looked upon him as being far too nice a gentleman to be able to control this large, outer London comprehensive school. Unfortunately his two deputies were similarly insignificant, so it really was a case of doing one's own thing. For me it worked.

However, indiscipline remained a serious problem culminating in union members of staff requesting a meeting with representatives of the Local Education Authority. In my opinion, this put a really good man under undue pressure. His only failure was his inability to adopt a positive role with both his staff and pupils. In other words, he was far too nice a gentleman to be in charge of a tough school with a somewhat militant staff.

Inevitably, this charming man reached retirement age and left. I remained at this school for fifteen years so, inevitably, encountered other newly appointed Heads and Deputies.

The next Head could not have been more different. For one thing she was a woman, highly qualified and ambitious. At first we all thought she would enhance the standards throughout. She introduced school uniform and appointed a new Deputy Head and a

Senior Teacher. However, the term "bitten off more than you can chew" soon seemed to apply to this lady.

She developed a knack of unwittingly upsetting members of staff — not least me. Perhaps, being a little jealous (or in awe) of my involvement with external examining, she called me into her office one day.

"I understand you hold several external examining posts."

Thinking I was about to be congratulated, I puffed out my chest and replied, "Yes. I'm chief examiner in various subjects for two boards and hold several assistant examiner posts."

"Well," she responded. "I've decided that this takes up far too much of your time, and I would like you to concentrate on, say, two of these posts and give up the rest."

I was flabbergasted but quick to respond. "I certainly will not. My contract of employment allows me ten days' leave of absence per year to attend meetings for this purpose and, so long as I do not exceed this, I consider that what posts I hold is my business and of no consequence to you or the school, except for the benefit my pupils receive from being taught by a member of staff who is conversant with the demands of the external examinations they sit and aware of future developments in these areas."

Fortunately, I knew that the Local Education Authority's Adviser for commercial subjects thought highly of me and my department. He had asked me to conduct various training courses for commercial teachers throughout the borough and held my department in high esteem, citing it as one of the largest and most successful in the area. I guessed he would support me should there be a confrontation with the Head over my attendance at meetings of examining boards.

To my surprise, the Head capitulated and never again questioned my involvement with activities outside the school.

Truth to tell, so keen was she to improve the status of the school within the borough and, no doubt, to further her own career, that she spent so much time outside the school interacting with VIPs and other influential people, that we, as a staff, were largely left to our own devises. However, one of her reasons for being out of school was, "I popped home to put a casserole in the oven." I wonder how she would have reacted should one of her staff have sought to do likewise!

My department was growing quite alarmingly. We now offered two "A" level subjects (Accounting and Economics) in addition to a full range of the office skills subjects and bookkeeping and commerce, all of which could be taken at relevant external examinations. In order to cater for all abilities, I also offered some non-examination courses one of which, Money Management, became popular and formed the basis of a CSE Mode 2 external examination.

The introduction of "A" level sociology to the school was muted, and it was decided to bring the course within my department since the department was already preparing pupils for social economics examinations. The Head informed me that she had taught "A" level sociology in the past and that she would like to be timetabled for this subject within my department. Although worried that her "out-of-school" demands might mean that the class was often left without a teacher, I was in no position to refuse her offer. As expected, she was seldom present to teach the pupils, setting work and expecting other staff to invigilate when they were free.

It was school policy for each department to hold regular departmental meetings. I always sent out a notice of meeting and agenda to the Head for my departmental meetings but, although strictly a member of my department, I cannot recall her ever attending.

Her monthly staff meetings were, on the other hand, obligatory. I term them "staff meetings" rather loosely, since they were more or less a lecture by the Head as to what was going to happen and what we were expected to do. There was little, if any, discussion. Heads of Departments meetings with the Head followed a similar pattern. They were merely a way of telling us what we had to do.

Being a person with lots of ideas, I found it very irksome being lectured at without the chance to put my point of view. One day I approached her and asked, "As your meetings are so one-sided, is it alright if I bring my knitting. I can assure you that I can listen and knit at the same time, and I do find a meeting which is so one-sided is rather a waste of my valuable time."

To my surprise, she agreed to my request, and I found that further staff and Heads of Department meetings were fruitful, if only in relation to my knitting.

It was decided that a new Faculty Head was needed. Being one of the longest-serving and more senior Heads of Departments, I considered applying for this post until the Head announced, "I want someone who is my intellectual equal to give me the stimulation I don't get at present. He, or she, must have a good degree from a good university. I don't want anyone on an ego trip."

Like me, most members of the existing staff decided not to apply. Fortunately this Head's reign was reasonably short-lived — approximately two years. However, during that period, the discipline of the school did not improve. Staff morale was low, since most felt they got no support from the Head. I had many disagreements with the lady, and on one occasion she described me as "abrasive and truculent." Maybe she was right in her judgement, but it was evident that one's ability to survive in this unhappy atmosphere depended on one's ability to set individual standards and stick to them.

So unhappy was I at this time that I considered a change of career. Instead I applied, was shortlisted and interviewed for Deputy Head of a neighbouring large comprehensive school. I felt the interview was going well but suddenly had doubts about my desire to come out of the classroom and into a more managerial and administrative post. I withdrew my application at this late stage only to learn, afterwards, that I had been the favoured candidate.

Back in my old school, we looked forward to a new, more inspiring Head. A dynamic man was appointed, well-known in the sporting field and showing signs of good managerial skills. This man did a lot for the school. Discipline was improved, and the school became popular within the borough, but he was not over enthusiastic about commercial subjects, and he and I soon clashed as regards the curriculum to be offered within my department.

By this time, I had introduced a scheme whereby adults from the local community could attend some of the sixth form secretarial lessons in order to learn, or improve, their office skills. This was quite a new initiative within the borough and proved to be most successful — eventually being copied by several other schools who offered adults the chance to attend lessons alongside pupils, not just in the commercial field.

However, a new type of GCSE was on offer for which there was some Department of Trade funding for any school which decided to offer it. From my external examining connections, I could see that this new examination would have several implications for my department. I would have to abandon my present examinable subjects and integrate them into this new double GCSE examination course which would not, to my mind, suitably prepare young people for careers in office work. As it happened, I was right to avoid this new examination. Although, at first, successful nationally, it eventually lost favour with the examination boards, probably because of its preponderance to lower standards.

However, such was my Head's desire to obtain extra funding, the course was earmarked as the only commercial course to be offered to GCSE Business Studies aspirants. My largest classroom — the one in which I normally taught, and which was used for the integrated adult/pupil courses — would have to be reorganised and refurbished. In all, I envisaged the destruction of all that I had built up over the past fourteen years at the school. Hence, I informed the Head that I was not in favour of this course and was not prepared to adopt it into my department.

He had other ideas. I was informed that I would accept his proposals or he would appoint someone else to conduct the new course. Even the local Advisor was unable to support me, and my refusal to have anything to do with the new course (which eventually did prove to be a failure for the school) meant that the Head appointed a new member of staff to take charge of the new course, albeit reluctantly, leaving me in my Head of Department role.

This new member of staff was an intelligent and amiable young lady who admitted to me that she did not have any faith in the course but was looking to enhance her career. She admitted to me that, at the interview for the post, she had "told them just what they wanted to hear."

The introduction of the course meant that I had to move from my large classroom into a smaller room totally inadequate for the number of typewriters I needed in order to teach the large adult classes. The new room had a small walk-in cupboard. I had a very large selection of equipment, consumables and sets of textbooks, the latter being housed on the wall-lined shelves.

During one lesson I was teaching in this "new" classroom, there was a distant rumbling sound and within seconds the door to the store cupboard burst open and scores of books and consumables spewed out across the floor. I continued teaching as though nothing had happened. It was something I had anticipated happening for some days since I had overloaded the shelves in my desperate search for storage space. The pupils all stopped what they were doing.

"Look, Miss, look what's happened in the store room."

"I know what has happened." I replied, "Take no notice. Get on with your work."

I was delighted to send for the Head at the end of the morning session so that he could view the results of his demanding that I be relegated to such a small room. He viewed the devastation and promptly resolved the situation by providing me with a carpenter who would put up more substantial shelves.

Needless-to-say, this new Head and I remained at variance in our ideas about the teaching of commercial subjects within the school, and I began to have to take time off through stress. In all, I considered this Head to be a typical bully. Several younger members were frightened of him, and there was little sense of cohesion among the staff. The Head was often away attending to his sporting activities, for which the Local Authority gave him leave of absence. During such times, the school ran quite successfully through its Deputies and senior staff.

For me, the joy of teaching was receding.

CHAPTER
ELEVEN

Time To Go

I have to admit that the latest Head to govern the school was a man for whom I had no respect. I found him arrogant, unsympathetic and a bully. His greatest failing was that he would not listen — a blow to me when other Heads had always granted me a hearing.

He made it very clear that, in his opinion, there were too many Heads of Department being paid on Scale 4, the highest salary for a classroom teacher. He let it be known that he wanted to economize on salaries and set about suggesting these Heads of Department (me included) considered taking early retirement.

The breaking up of my department through the introduction of the new course against my will, meant I was finding the job more and more stressful and not at all rewarding.

During a spell off sick with glandular fever, I contemplated early retirement albeit only one year early since I was nearly 59 years of age.

I think my decision must have come as a welcome relief for the Head, as he set things in motion so that, by the summer of 1989, I had taken early retirement and been replaced by a young male teacher on the lower Scale 3 salary. Indeed the Head's plans were falling into place.

My departure from the school was acrimonious. I felt the Head made life so difficult for me — imposing a new course, taking away my large classroom, denying me access to a phone, appointing staff without my advice or input and effectively halving the areas over which I had jurisdiction — that my leaving the school could have been seen as constructive dismissal. But I had been ill and was feeling my age. I had seen my large department, which had taken years of hard work to build up, shattered. I had no support from the top management and, frankly, all the fight had gone out of me. I had hoped for support from the local Adviser since I had, in the past, helped him by running training courses for probationary teachers, but it was not to be. I didn't stay to fight for compensation through constructive dismissal but, to the Head's delight, went quietly.

I left at the end of summer term 1989 whilst I was still home on sick leave. The Head sent a very short letter of appreciation and a small cheque from the staff. Not much for fifteen years of loyal service!

However, as a divorcee with a mortgage, I had to think about getting another job. Would it be in teaching or should I try another career?

CHAPTER
TWELVE

Full Circle

Although I had finished teaching during the day, I still had evening classes. I taught shorthand, typewriting and business studies. My classes were always in demand, and I enjoyed the social side of being involved with adults.

I was enjoying more and more work as an external examiner which was financially lucrative but did not bring in the constant salary so necessary to cover my mortgage and other expenses. I could not face returning to teaching so, whilst out shopping one day, I passed an employment agency advertising for a Secretary. I went in and enquired:

"Have you any use for a geriatric shorthand typist secretary?"

A rather bemused interviewer suggested that there might be a vacancy in the local office of an international airfreight company. Apparently the Director of Transport had interviewed several young ladies but had not found any suitable.

I set about taking a shorthand typing test and found I had lost none of my office skills despite having used them only infrequently for the past forty years.

Fortunately I did not look my age, and the kindly interviewer telephoned the client, explaining that I was fifty-nine years old but that she felt he ought to consider me. I went for an interview and was asked to take down a piece of shorthand and transcribe it on an electronic typewriter — few computers were in use at this time. I have never come across such a contrived piece of dictation. It contained just about all the difficult and often misspelt words one could think of. I duly transcribed the work and took it in to the Director for checking. I was amused to hear him say, "Did you have any difficulty with spelling? Did you use a dictionary?" I answered, "No" to both questions and then chuckled to myself, as I noticed he had to refer to a correct transcription to ensure I did, in fact, have no spelling errors.

"You are just what I am looking for," he announced. "You are the first person to give me a perfectly spelt transcript. You wouldn't believe some of the rubbish I have seen. When can you start."

Although the salary was less than that of a probationary teacher, I was delighted to feel appreciated and started work the next day.

The job was interesting. Dealing with international companies was demanding, especially as I did not speak a foreign language. A geographical filing system took me back to the first office job I had had when I got married, that of secretary to a metal exporter. That office used a geographical filing system too. It took some time to come to terms with airfreight jargon, but I learned a lot and was one of the few secretaries who had already had some experience of computers when they were introduced to the office.

I must say I enjoyed my re-entry into my original career in office work. Although the hours were longer than in teaching (9a.m. to 5.30p.m. with one hour for lunch) the job was much less demanding.

As my boss was in charge of freight being transported all over the world, communications were interesting to say the least. I became quite ashamed to admit that, like most British people, I did not speak foreign languages. However, it seemed that whatever firm I needed to telephone, in whatever country, contacts were always available who spoke English. All written correspondence was in English.

In teaching office practice over the past thirty odd years, I had encountered, and taught theoretically, the new innovations in communications, mainly Telex and fax. Now I had to use these methods. It took no time at all to put theory into practice. I even successfully programmed the fax machine with all the important international contacts — a job many employees had been asked to do, but none was brave enough to attempt.

I shared an office with two other senior secretaries both middle-aged, long-serving employees. I was accepted, somewhat sceptically at first, and worked happily alongside them despite a rather dark and forbidding environment, for the office had no windows, so we worked all day in artificial light.

However, I was having to take days off from my annual leave to attend the odd external examiner's meeting and kept waiting for a half term holiday, which, of course, didn't come. By Christmas, I had had enough of office hours and lack of holidays, so I chose to return to teaching by way of supply work.

I enjoyed a couple of interesting term appointments, covering for teachers on maternity leave.

In one such appointment, I was forced to teach the double GCSE combined business studies course which I had refused to adopt in my own school and which had resulted in my retirement.

The six month temporary contract at this school convinced me that my decision had been correct. Pupils were not motivated by this course which was based on a series of investigative coursework projects. It took all my efforts, during class times, to stop less interested pupils using the computers to play games. Little work was done. Groups were noisy, and discussion seemed to centre around any topic other than business studies. Yet coursework seemed to be miraculously completed by the end of the term usually when completed as homework, the authentication of which was highly questionable.

However, such placements were not close to home and, once again, I found travelling over an hour each way to school somewhat irksome. I found a permanent part-time post teaching business studies in a small comprehensive school nearer home. Here I got more experience in teaching computer studies since, by this time, typewriters had been superseded by computers. The staff at the school was friendly and part-time work suited me admirably.

I was able to develop the department a little and started teaching "A" level business studies with great success. My successful pupils were the first in the school to get places in university to study business management and allied courses.

But fate was against me, and the school was deemed surplus to local requirements and closed down. What was I to do?

I took a long look at my finances and determined that, at the age of sixty-three and with my mortgage now paid off, I could afford to concentrate on my two main interests: external examining and writing.

Within a year of abandoning classroom teaching, I was adamant that I would never return to the classroom — but I had enjoyed my teaching years and gained much satisfaction from them.

I count myself lucky to have enjoyed such varied experiences in my teaching career. The changes during my forty-year career were extensive but each brought challenges and satisfaction. My pupils' successes and frequent appreciation were reward enough.

Also available in ISIS Large Print:

Early Bird

Richard Mack

"I had been involved with farming for most of my life, so I thought I could cope with the early start — though rising at 4a.m. did seem a little extreme"

Early Bird is a tongue-in-cheek tale based on the author's fifteen-year stint as a postman. By turns humorous and disrespectful, the author takes us on a journey into the world of Royal Mail — introducing us to the eccentricities of its arcane working practices, its employees, its customers and their dogs.

Prior to his employment as a postman, the author was already an Early Bird. Throughout this book he brings us delightful yarns of his past life as a market gardener/farmer and other country cameos.

The market town of Bramton could be anywhere in England, and the characters therein could be found in many a rural locality. The story starts one dark, August morning at 4a.m.

ISBN 978-0-7531-8402-8 (hb)
ISBN 978-0-7531-8403-5 (pb)

Memoirs of a Cotswold Vet

Ivor Smith

"When the telephone rang at 11p.m. that night the last thing I imagined I would hear was, "For Christ's sake get here quick mister, he's grown another bleedin' leg!""

This heart-warming account of veterinary life traces Ivor Smith's early days as a student at university through setting up his own practice in the Cotswolds, recounting a memorable 40 years in the profession. Following in the Herriot tradition of veterinary humour, Ivor's memories of life as a vet in a very mixed practice include hilarious incidents, colourful local characters and engaging patients. From calving cows in the middle of cold spring nights and handling ferocious gerbils, to setting up home in a mouse-infested farmhouse, and even finding a new-born baby on his doorstep, Ivor shares his respect for animals and joy of the beautiful Cotswold countryside in this entertaining read.

ISBN 978-0-7531-8386-1 (hb)
ISBN 978-0-7531-8387-8 (pb)